The Italian Heritage Tours
A Fun and Easy Way to Discover Italy

by Remo Faieta, Ph.D.

DORRANCE
PUBLISHING CO
EST. 1920
PITTSBURGH, PENNSYLVANIA 15238

The contents of this work, including, but not limited to, the accuracy of events, people, and places depicted; opinions expressed; permission to use previously published materials included; and any advice given or actions advocated are solely the responsibility of the author, who assumes all liability for said work and indemnifies the publisher against any claims stemming from publication of the work.

Dorrance Publishing Co
585 Alpha Drive
Suite 103
Pittsburgh, PA 15238
Visit our website at *www.dorrancebookstore.com*

ISBN: 978-1-4809-4690-3
eISBN: 978-1-4809-4713-9

TURIN

MILAN

VENICE

GENUA

BOLOGNA

PISA

FLORENCE

ASSISI

ABRUZZO

CAMPOBASSO

ROME

FOGGIA

BARI

NAPLES

POTENZA

CALABRIA

COSENZA

CATANZARO

SARDINIA

PALERMO

MESSINA

SICILY

CATANIA

AGRIGENTO

CONTENTS

INTRODUCTION

It was a pleasure for me to read this book. It brought back memories and visions of so many places of the beautiful land I left fifty-five years ago. This book surpasses all the other books about tourism to Italy, because it is a true experience of life full of information on history, geography, arts, literature, religion, cuisine, fashion, local traditions, and family roots. Most of all, this book shows very clearly how relaxing, enjoyable and safe it is to discover "Bella Italia" with an escorted group tour.

Through all the lines of this wonderful book, the Reader will appreciate the Author's love for Italy and his enjoyment in presenting it to us. In reading it, one feels as though he/she is on a live tour of Italy. Yes, this book shows you what other books only tell you.

Beginning the day of landing in Milan and then for the next fifteen days, Dr. Remo Faieta, a native of Italy, enthusiastically leads his group of "good people" through the major Italian tourist places. What a wonderful and unique experience to learn about the beauty of the Alpine Lake Maggiore, the wealthy city of Milan, the fairy-tale Venice, the pilgrims of Padua, the glorious Florence and its Renaissance, the still Leaning Tower of Pisa, the Tuscan olive orchards, vineyards and wineries, Assisi and its Franciscan spirit, the lost and found city of Pompeii, the enchanted Isle of Capri, the grandeur of Rome of the Caesars and the heart of the Christendom in Vatican City! Yes, all those places and many more come alive in this book. After reading, one feels a visit to Italy is a dream that must come true.

Moreover, Dr. Faieta's activity is not limited to the usual Italian tourist places. He takes his people to the remote mountain towns of central and southern Italy, where no other tour goes. Those towns are dear to many Italian-Americans, because it is where their family roots begin. Chapter 12 of this book describes the moment when a few of those travelers meet their "lost relatives" for the first time. It is an emotional event that brings tears to everybody's eyes. Not only, but to see the locals' kindness, to observe their simple, daily life and enjoy their food and wine is a pleasant and unforgettable highlight of the tour.

In particular, I like the description Dr. Faieta gives about the "spirit of friendship" his vacationers develop during his escorted tours. He states that, although people in the group come from different parts of the country, during the first days of the tour they all become "buddy, as if they had known each other for a longtime." Faieta explains: "Making new friends, eating, drinking, laughing, dancing, singing, walking with them and visiting interesting places with a total peace of mind: that is a real pleasurable and enjoyable vacation!" The Reader actually feels that happy spirit in each page of this book. No wonder at the conclusion of the tour Faieta's "good sheep" assure him: "It was a trip of a life-time. We enjoyed every single bit of it. Italy has become part of my soul." Let us not forget the bus driver, Signor Mariano. Faieta always starts him as "Corporal Mariano", but, because he is a very safe driver, courteous with his passengers, and keeps his deluxe bus always spotless, people quickly promote him to "Captain Mariano!"

ORAZIO TANELLI
University Professor
Verona, New Jersey. USA

PREFACE

Because of its natural beauty and historic, religious and artistic heritage, Italy is a major tourist destination. People from all over the world travel to "Bella Italia" with enthusiasm and expectations of an enjoyable experience. The success of that experience depends on how well they plan their trip.

To make their journey enjoyable, people must make proper arrangements for air and land transportation; they must choose nice places to visit, reserve fine hotels and good restaurants and, most of all, they need to know how much their Italian adventure will cost.

That is not easy to do and traveling to Italy as inexperienced individuals is a risky adventure that could become a nightmare. Whereas, traveling with an Escorted Group Tour presents no concerns at all, because the tour is planned and conducted by professionals. With an Escorted Group Tour, people will know in advance the details of the tour, the name of the hotels and how much it will cost. Moreover, it is much safer to travel with a group. That peace of mind is essential for a truly enjoyable vacation.

The purpose of this book is to provide the Reader with a complete day-by-day overview of what an Escorted Group Tour to Italy with the Italian Heritage Tours is all about and the great satisfaction associated with it.

CHAPTER 1

ITALY, A VACATIONER'S PARADISE

If on a clear summer night we look at the sky we might see hundreds of bright stars, but we know there are countless more in the heavens. In the immensity of the Universe, our planet Earth is like a grain of sand on the beach. Yet, as far we know, that one grain of sand is the most beautiful and hospitable of all planets. Just think of the sky with its towering clouds, gentle rain and powerful wind. Picture the sea with its many creatures and the land with its majestic mountains, scenic rivers and lakes, green hills and wide plains. Add the beauty of flowers in spring, summer with its golden fields, autumn with colorful leaves and winter with a blanket of white snow. It becomes obvious the Creator of the Universe made Earth a special place to host a special guest: mankind. Yes, Dear Reader, that guest is you and I. Not only, but He gave us the *intelligence* to discover and use everything on Earth to constantly improve our living.

Dante Alighieri, the greatest Italian poet, reminded us:

"Fatti non foste per viver come bruti, ma per seguir virtute e conoscenza."

(*You were not made to live like brutes, but to pursue virtue and knowledge*).

In his pursuit of knowledge Man is eager to find out which part of his earthly kingdom is most beautiful. For that purpose let's imagine we are circling our planet in a spaceship. Immediately, an unusual piece of land in the middle of the Mediterranean Sea catches our attention. It is shaped like a boot; it looks like a bridge connecting Europe with Africa; it has borders well-defined by the sea on three sides and by a crown of majestic mountains, the Alps, on the north; it has blue lakes, clear rivers, picturesque valleys, wide fields of grain, vineyards and olive groves. You guessed correctly: that unique piece of land is *Italia* (Italy).

Now let us take a closer look at that magical land. Have you seen the Alps and the soul-stirring Dolomites? Did you visit the Italian Riviera? Have you seen the Tuscan countryside? Have you been to the Amalfi Coast? Imagine: when the inhabitants of Amalfi and Capri die and go to Heaven, they look around and say:

"Well, nothing new. It looks just like home!"

You will be amazed when you see the sunny, warm, and pristine Italian beaches. What about the Italian weather? The air is always pure, the sky blue and the sun shining; winters are mild and summers temperate.

No wonder many poets and famous travelers called Italy *The Tourist's Paradise, The Bel Paese, The Beautiful Country by excellence.* Tourists coming back from Italy confirm: "Once you have been to beautiful Italy you will forget the other lands."

To that natural beauty we must add Italy has been the cradle of Western Civilization: the Roman culture, language, law, civil engineering, art, architecture, administrative, and military might united people from England to Egypt and from Spain to the Russian shores. Moreover, after a long period of medieval Dark Ages, civilization was born again in Italy with the *Renaissance.*

Yes, it is a fascinating experience to discover Italy, but until very recently the world did not have that opportunity. It was hard to travel on horseback and carriage for weeks or months just for the pleasure of seeing those beautiful places. There were no convenient roads, motels and restaurants on the way! It is only recently fast trains, freeways, airplanes, hotels and improved economic conditions have made it possible for people to discover and enjoy Italy.

Looking at post-cards of Rome as recent as 1950s, I see only a few tourists around the Coliseum and St. Peter's Square. Old post-cards of Venice show only a few honeymooners having fun feeding pigeons on St. Mark Square. In the early 1960s when I was a university student in Rome, tourists were such a rarity that when Roman men saw a pretty American woman, they sighed: "Che Bella! Che Carina!" (How pretty! How lovely!). They always found a way to *pinch* her *cheeks*.

The next time I returned to Rome in the late 1970s, there were so many tourists those gallant Romans had no time for sighing and pinching: they were all busy serving pizza, spaghetti, and wine! Yes, within the last fifty years there has been a real explosion of tourist activity and Italy has been invaded by vacationers. Today, the Roman streets have more visitors than cobblestones; the crowds of tourists in Florence outnumbers those of the locals and the Venetian pigeons can hardly find a place to land among the crowd of tourists on St. Mark Square.

Exactly, what draws people from around the world to Italy? They are enticed by its breathtaking natural beauty, its stunning beaches, its unparalleled cultural heritage, its splendid arts and monuments, its outstanding history, its famous religious sites, mild weather, elegant fashion, delicious food and friendly people. Many people are also motivated by the discovery of their Italian family roots.

Yes, today, to visit *Bella Italia* has become everybody's dream. The only question people have is this: "*When* and *how* can I make that dream come true?"

When? The best time is to go during your "vacation". In fact, the term "vacation" comes from the Latin verb "vacare" and it means "to vacate, to make empty". Therefore to go on vacation and enjoy it one has to "vacate, make empty" his/her mind of the daily concerns and fill it with *new and pleasurable* things. Oh, for sure Italy has plenty of new and pleasurable things to offer the visitors!

How to visit Italy? Dear Reader, I see you too are anxious to have that dream come true. Perhaps you have already consulted a travel agency and a few books; perhaps you have browsed the Internet for information, but you are still pondering: "Should I go to Italy by myself or should I join an escorted group tour?" I suggest that, unless you are an expert traveler, you should not go by yourself, because your dream vacation might turn out to be disappointing, very expensive and, most of all, you might miss discovering the Italian wonders you wanted to see and enjoy. I strongly recommend you join an *escorted group tour because with it you will have complete peace of mind*, which is essential for a "pleasurable" vacation. On an escorted tour, you know exactly what you will see, which hotels you will stay, how you will travel, and how much your vacation will cost. You will have an expert *escort* who explains everything and makes sure you are safe. Moreover, you will love the spirit of friendship you will develop with people in your group. Discovering new and interesting places with total peace of mind, eating, drinking, laughing, dancing, singing, walking together with your fellow travelers, and making new friends: that for sure is a real *pleasurable* vacation!

Dear Reader, using your imagination, now please join my vacationers and find out what an Escorted Tour to Bella Italia with the Italian Heritage Tours is all about. You will feel like you were on tour in Italy with us. (1)

---

(1) Most people, when planning a vacation to Italy, go to a bookstore, browse anxiously the *Travel Section,* and eventually buy a sort of *guidebook*. Yes, guidebooks do contain a large amount of information about how to get there, how to get around, where to stay, what to see, where to eat, where to shop, etc. In fact, they contain such a large description of those topics and so many pictures the Reader becomes quite confused. For instance, during the couple days a traveler spends in Rome or Florence, he/she is certainly not going to see the myriad things described in the guidebook he/she bought. It would take days to do that! As a result, the inexpert traveler is still confused and ponders:

"Among all those topics (where to stay, what to see, where to eat…), what should I choose?"

It is important to understand that this book, *The Italian Heritage Tours*, is not a guidebook. People in an escorted group tour don't need a guidebook because they have their own *live guide!* The purpose of this book is to give the reader a good overview of the most important tourist attractions he/she will actually see during the visit to the major places described hereafter. He/she will also have a taste of the great peace of mind and enjoyment associated with an escorted group tour.

Amalfi Coast

CHAPTER 2

JOINING AN ESCORTED GROUP TOUR TO ITALY

Mrs. Karen Gentile from Pittsburgh, PA, had heard stories from her grandparents about Italy and the quaint town of Pettorano sul Gizio they had left behind in Abruzzo, a mountain region east of Rome. For years she imagined it as a magic land she dreamed of visiting. She spent hours reading books and watching movies about Italy. One day, as she told her co-workers about the unfulfilled dream, Josephine shared the joy of a fabulous trip to Italy she recently took. A few days later, she showed Karen several pictures of that trip. Josephine said she traveled with a tour company called the *Italian Heritage Tours* located in a suburb of Columbus, Ohio. Karen became very excited and resolved she would go to Italy as soon as she retired.

In early March 2012, Karen called me and inquired: "Hello, this is Karen Gentile. I heard very good things about your tours and I would like to have some information. Could you send me some literature? Do you still have room for two people in your September tour?"

Her call was immediately answered: "Hello, Karen. This is *Remo,* the owner of the Italian Heritage Tours. Yes, I do have a few more seats available. I will be very happy to have you in my tour. The brochure describing the tours will be in the mail tomorrow morning."

Karen received the brochure, read it with enthusiasm and decided: "Yes, this is the perfect tour! It goes to all the places I want to see, including Abruzzo. The price is very reasonable." She called Remo again: "Sir, I read your brochure. My husband, Tony, and I are very interested. What do we need to do to join your tour?"

"Grazie, Karen. To join the tour, please send a deposit of $500 each."

With her deposit, Karen included a note: "We are anxiously looking forward to our trip." As soon as I received the deposit, I entered Karen's and Tony's data into the appropriate records and mailed them a two-page "Receipt-Letter" in which I confirmed their reservation and listed important information to prepare for the tour. I specified the date for her last payment. I also included a brochure for travel insurance handled by a reputable insurance company. "Cancellation insurance is not obligatory, but very wise," I explained.

About twenty days later, Karen called again: "Buon Giorno, Remo. Come stai? (Good morning, Remo. How are you?) I have been studying Italian! Do you have room for two more people? Two of my lady friends decided to join us."

"Si, Signora Karen. I do have room for your two friends. I welcome them too. Grazie."

Winter was gone, spring flowers bloomed, and birds sang in the trees. As time for the tour neared, everyone became more excited. By the end of May, everybody had paid in full for their trip. I had thirty-five people very anxious to leave for Italy. They were from several parts of the USA: Ohio, Pennsylvania, Texas, Missouri, Florida, West Virginia, Indiana, New York, Maryland, and Arizona.

In early July, I mailed the airline tickets, the list of people in the group, a list of hotels, and a few pages of useful information. I explained about the flight, meeting the group, hotel rooms, baggage handling, breakfasts, dinners, drinks, riding the bus, safety tips, and other valuable information. In early September, my vacationers prepared their suitcases. A few ladies called me with last minute questions.

"How many pieces of luggage are we allowed on the plane?"

"How many pounds can we have?"

"Should we change money now or in Italy?"

"Do they have hair-dryers in the hotels?"

"Is their electric power 110 or 220 watts?"

"Do we need to have a voltage converter and a plug adapter?"

"Do they have wash clothes in bathrooms?"

"Is their water safe to drink?"

"What if I cannot sleep on the eve of departure?"

I explained the airline allows only one suitcase per person with a maximum of fifty pounds and one small carry-on, all hotels have hairdryers, and it would be convenient to have some euros before leaving. "If you cannot sleep, count sheep for an hour or drink some good Italian wine!"

September 14, 2012 finally arrived. Karen Gentile woke up at 6:00 a.m. got dressed, and drank two cups of coffee before waking up Tony at 8:30 a.m. He jumped out of bed and sang, "*O Sole Mio! Santa Lucia*!" At 9:30 a.m., they took a taxi to Pittsburgh Airport. They checked their baggage through Milan, Italy, and at 2:35 p.m. landed in Philadelphia. Since they were inexpert travelers, they asked for directions here and there and finally made it to Gate D17. Karen's dream was about to come true.

I always escort my group tours to Italy. Of my thirty-five travelers, I had met only a few. When I arrived at Philadelphia International Airport, I went straight to Gate D17. There, I found more than 200 people waiting to go to Milan. Some of them were sitting, some standing, several browsing in the food stands, some talking, a few were watching planes landing and taking off, some were eating and others sleeping. Two young ladies had an inscription on their carry-on bags, "Italy or Bust!" Which travelers belonged to my flock? I was not sure. Since I had informed them to look for a dapper man holding a *red carnation* atop an antenna, as I raised that sign, several smiling people got up and greeted me:

"Ciao! You must be Remo. Glad to meet you."

Time quickly passed as I answered a few questions:

"At what time do we get to Milan?"

"Why was my plane from Sarasota late?"

"Are they going to feed us on the plane?"

"Where is the rest of the group sitting on the plane?"

"Will we see the Pope?"

"How is the weather in Milan?"

"Is our bus air-conditioned?"

"Are we really going to a winery?"

"Are figs and grapes ripe now in Italy?"

"Will we see the catacombs?"

"Is it true in Italy they don't serve meatballs with spaghetti?"

At 17:45 p.m., a loud voice came from Desk D17. "Ladies and Gentlemen, now we'll begin to board the plane for Milan. Passengers in Zone A, please come forth and show your ticket and passport."

Everybody, even those who were sleeping, came alive and lined up. Orderly and smiling, all passengers went through the checkpoint and walked onto the airplane. They placed their carry-on baggage in the overhead compartment, sat in their assigned seats and remained silent. A certain apprehension of flying could be read on a few faces.

At 18:30, a firm voice from the cockpit announced: "Good evening, gadies and gentlemen, and welcome aboard! This is your captain, George Miller. Please, make yourself comfortable and remain seated. We will take off very shortly."

A flight attendant explained the safety rules, and soon we were on the runway. A sudden rumble of powerful engines indicated we were taking off. Some people made the sign of cross and prayed silently. Since I was sitting by a window, I could see the city of Philadelphia disappearing very quickly down below. Then, a large, fluffy cloud covered everything; the clouds were like tufts of cotton which then turned into blankets of cotton. A few minutes later, the sky above became clear; the airplane flew above the clouds and I enjoyed a spectacular sunset on the horizon. When we reached the cruising altitude of 37,000 ft., the courteous flight attendants served dinner.

"Do you want pasta or chicken?" they asked each person. Most people ate chicken, but the Italians preferred pasta.

"Do we get wine too? How much costs?" Joe asked.

"Sir, it is five dollars."

"Five dollars for a glass of wine! No, thank you. Tomorrow, in Italy, I can get a gallon of wine for that price!"

With pasta or chicken, we also had salad, a roll, mashed potatoes, crackers, cheese, and brownies. After dinner, some people watched movies on a TV screen; others fell asleep and some were quite annoying with their loud snoring. In the meantime, the plane continued over eastern Canada, and then over the Atlantic Ocean.

During the night, I dozed now and then, but it was not easy to sleep, being confined into a narrow seat. A couple of hours later, I opened the blind, looked outside, and saw a very thin, pinkish light on the faraway horizon; it was dawn. It was a dream-like vision. I checked my watch; it was only 11:00 p.m. I tried to sleep again.

At about 1:00 a.m., all lights were turned on in the airplane. People woke up. Some got up and stretched their arms; there was a line to the bathroom. Breakfast was soon served. Breakfast at 1:00 a.m.! Yes, but it was 7:00 a.m. in Italy. We had croissants, bananas, orange juice, granola bars, coffee, or tea.

The plane flew over England, Northern France, and Switzerland. As we flew over the Alps, the lucky people sitting by the window enjoyed a breathtaking view. The sky was clear and a blanket of fresh snow could be seen over most of the alpine peaks.

Just as the airplane began its descent, the Po Valley became visible. The head stewardess asked everyone to remain seated and to fasten their seat-belts. Captain Miller announced: "Ladies and Gentlemen, in a few minutes we will land in Milan. Welcome to Italy, and thank you for flying US Airways."

A loud applause from all passengers sounded in the airplane as the wheels touched ground. Some passengers were heard saying, "Thank You, Lord!"

We landed at *Malpensa International Airport* at 8:15 a.m., and that meant 2:15 a.m. New York time. We said good-bye to those sitting by us, and then stood in line for passport control.

"Oh, look at those young policemen, aren't they cute?" remarked a couple of giddy young ladies. We proceeded to the baggage claim, picked up our luggage, and walked through customs. No questions were asked. The customs officers smiled at us and we smiled at them.

Group of Vacationers in Assisi

CHAPTER 3

THE WONDERFUL ALPINE REGION

The arrival Hall of Malpensa's Airport is huge; its ceiling soars overhead. There, I raised my red carnation and my good people gathered around me. Although exhausted, they looked at me with enthusiasm and excitement. Some asked:

"Where is the bathroom?"

"Do I have time to change some money?"

"Do I have time for a cappuccino?"

"Where is the bus?"

"Is everybody here?"

"Do we have far to walk to the bus?"

"What time will we get to the hotel?"

"What time is dinner?"

Mary, an attractive, single lady in my group, came close to me and whispered: "Remo, you have beautiful, twinkling blue eyes. Are you really from Italy?"

I kindly responded, "Grazie, Maria." At the same time, I looked around and thought: *I hope no one heard her!* I pulled the group list from my briefcase and roll-called. When everybody was accounted for, I shouted, "Okay. Everyone is here. Now follow me to the bus!"

My *good sheep* grabbed their baggage and followed me with firm steps, like soldiers marching on a parade. The walk to the bus parking lot was short. I instructed everyone to leave all baggage on both sides of the bus, to take a seat inside, and relax.

Except for a few couples, this group of tourists did not know each other. They sat on the bus silently and smiling. Being more than 4000 miles away from home, it appeared they'd just landed on another planet. When they heard me speaking Italian with the bus driver, they were amazed and thought I was kind of like Superman.

I entered the bus, picked up the microphone, faced the crowd, and said, "Buon Giorno a tutti (Good morning, everybody) and welcome to Bella Italia! How nice to see all these smiling faces! I am Remo, your tour director. I will be with you for the rest of the tour. And this gentleman is *Corporal Mariano,* our bus driver." I liked to tease Mariano by calling him *Corporal,* but later people promoted him to *Captain Mariano.* His bus was only six months old and it had lovely royal blue and white plush seats. For the next several days, that bus became *our home away from home.*

There was an immediate response from the group:

"Hello, Remo! Buon Giorno, Mariano!"

I told Mariano: "Ci siamo. Andiamo." (Everyone is here. Let us go). The bus started rolling and our great *Tour of Italy* began. It was about 9:45 a.m.

Malpensa International Airport is at about one hour drive north of Milan. Since people were weary after a sleepless night, it was not wise to visit busy downtown Milan. On the other hand, we could not check into our hotel before 2:00 p.m. Therefore, we spent a few leisure hours in the resort Alpine town of *Stresa,* located by the *Lago Maggiore* (Major Lake).

As soon as we left the airport and hit the freeway, I explained, "Italy is about the size of California and has a population of sixty million people. The country is divided into twenty *regions.* Each region is similar to a state. Now we are traveling through the Lombardia region. The mountains you see ahead of us are the Pre-Alps, and the snow-capped peaks on the far background are the Alps." People listened attentively and smiled at me.

Our Grand Tourism Bus

After a short ride through a wooded area, our bus crossed the Ticino River and entered the Piemonte Region. A few minutes later, we left the freeway, drove through the town of Arona, and then along the southernmost shores of *Lago Maggiore,* one of the prettiest Alpine lakes with many dream like panoramic views. Its waters reflect the distant mountains, near villages, and lakeside villas. The lake extends for about forty-five miles. The locals call it "The lake where wishes come true." The radiance of the setting, the pleasantness of the temperate climate, and the exuberance of the Mediterranean vegetation amazed my visitors. Although that enchanting lake is on the same latitude as upstate New York, palm trees, azaleas, camellias, rhododendrons, magnolias, giant sequoias, lemon trees, olive trees, chestnut forests, and exotic plants can be seen everywhere.

As we entered the shore of Lago Maggiore, everybody became thrilled, even those who were napping came alive. I preferred to stop talking and to listen to their comments and questions:

"It is fantastic!"

"Look at the deep, blue water!"

"How deep is it?"

"Are there fish in the lake?"

"Can we take a boat ride on this lake?"

"Look at those little, lovely villages!"

"Look at the beautiful villas on the shore!"

"How much does a villa like that cost?"

"Look at those huge pine trees!"

"Look at those palm trees!"

"There are even fig trees here!"

"Look at the exotic plants!"

"Look at the fascinating lakeside setting and its neat towns!"

"Oh, this is unique! I am so happy I came on this tour!"

"Look at those outdoor cafés along the water!"

"Does it snow here in winter?"

"I am surprised how neat and clean the streets and gardens are."

"What are those islands in the lake?"

I did my best to answer all questions, but how could I know everything? I could not quote the exact depth of the lake and the height of each mountain peak. I knew the majestic, snowcapped *Monte Rosa* in the background was 15,200 feet high and the Matterhorn 14,692 feet.

Sometimes I responded jokingly: "Oh, this lake it is very, very deep. That mountain is very, very high!" I also explained the Alps shield the area from the cold northern winds and the water of the lake keeps a mild temperature all year around. I described the beauty of the three islands in the lake. "Those are like three gems dropped into the blue lake. *Isola Bella* (Beautiful Island) is unequaled for its beauty and luxuriant tropical vegetation where peacocks, parrots, and pheasants roam wild; *Isola Madre* (Mother Island) has impressive gardens and *Isola dei Pescatori* (Fisherman's Island) has more restaurants than residents." Oh my, the tour was just beginning!

Mariano, concentrated on driving the bus through the winding road around the lake, then he turned to me and said, "The great surprise is coming." As he made another turn, there was Stresa, known as *The Pearl* and *The Queen of Lago Maggiore*.

Immediately, everybody sighed, "Oh, look at that! What a beautiful place!"

Yes, Stresa is one of the world's most popular and beautiful tourist destinations. It is a picturesque, peaceful, and romantic resort town of about 5,000 inhabitants. It has marvelous gardens growing rare and exotic plants. Visitors enjoy its wonderful promenades along the lake, spectacular views, elegant hotels, shops, and restaurants.

Our bus stopped in Piazza Marconi, right by the lake. When everyone was out of the bus, I said, "Right across the street, you can find a few banks for changing your money into euros. Walk a little further and you will see *Piazza Cadorna*; that is the city center. There, you will find outdoor cafés where you can have tasty food and enjoy watching people. Be back here by the lake at 1:30 p.m."

Just like timid rabbits in an open field, each person left the group, crossed main street and, hesitantly, but happy, spread throughout the quaint streets of Stresa. They did some window-shopping and found everything beautiful.

Piazza Cadorna is surrounded by palaces, which still retain the aristocratic glamour of the *belle epoque*. For centuries, numerous illustrious European writers, artists and intellectuals, including Byron, Wagner, and Goethe, chose Stresa for their summer residence. The piazza is still a favorite place for tourists to shop and eat. Large, green beech trees provide shade. There are many quaint shops, cafés, and restaurants with inside and outside tables. The tables have large umbrellas, comfortable chairs, colorful clothes, smoking pizzas, and cheerful people. Everything was so inviting. The waiters rushed back and forth, carrying trays balanced on one hand.

I walked to Piazza Cadorna and saw many people eating pizza and drinking espresso or wine. Some of them smiled at me, and that was the only way I knew they were part of my group.

Joe called, "Remo, how do I say in Italian: 'Please, waiter, I would like a glass of red wine'?"

"Cameriere, per favore vorrei un bicchiere di vino rosso."

"Yes, sir. Right away!" the waiter answered immediately.

"Why bother saying anything it in Italian? It seems everybody here understands English, even the girl at the bank," remarked Joe's wife. I stopped at Café' Marisa and had my favorite *panino* (sandwich) with prosciutto, mozzarella, olive oil, lettuce, and tomato. It was *delizioso*! (delicious).

Time passed quickly, and at 1:30 p.m. everybody was by the bus or walking along the waterfront feeding the fish and ducks with biscuits. I called the roll and Mariano drove us along the lake, and then up on a scenic mountain road. The view below became more beautiful with breathtaking Alpine scenery, unspoiled nature and picturesque villages.

Our four-star *Hotel Tre Laghi* (Three Lakes Hotel) was in the neat town of *Nebbiuno*. When we arrived, the staff was waiting for us. The *Rooming List* was on the desk, and all rooms were assigned within minutes. Smiling and gracious, Alberto, the hotel owner, shook everybody's hand as he gave us the key to our rooms. Using the elevator, one by one, people and their baggage disappeared upstairs.

When I arrived to my room, I walked to the balcony and, to my surprise, I saw I was not the only one enjoying the wonderful view. Most people were on their balconies looking down the mountain and making comments.

"Look how nice! What a breathtaking view! It reminds me of the mountains in the movie 'The Sound of Music'."

"I can see three lakes from here."

"Look at those palm trees right under my window!"

"Hello, Remo! Well done!"

"I know Italy is a nice place, but this is above my expectations!"

"Remo, let's stay here for the rest of the tour!"

Despite all the enthusiasm, about thirty minutes later, everybody was sleeping. Fortunately, I asked Alberto to wake us up at 7:00 p.m.; there was a risk someone could fall asleep for the rest of the night and miss the first delicious Italian dinner.

At 7:30 p.m., my hungry ladies and gentlemen came to the hotel's restaurant. Some ladies, dressed like queens, descended the stairs smiling to everyone. We sat in comfortable chairs and the Maître D asked his waiters to start serving dinner. Four handsome, young men dressed in white uniforms brought dishes of freshly cooked spaghetti. They did not talk, but served promptly with a smile and bow. Cheese was on the table and we used all of it. Most people cut their spaghetti in little pieces, but those of Italian descent laughed and showed how to roll them with a spoon and a fork.

There were six people at each table. Most of them introduced themselves and soon became *buddies*, as if they had known each other for a longtime. Soon, laughter and comments about the food began.

"This is the best pasta I ever ate!"

"It is really *al dente*!"

"The sauce is just like my grandmother used to make!"

"I love this wine! Remo, is wine included?"

I explained that wine usually is not included in the cost of the tour, unless it is already on the table. At Hotel Tre Laghi, wine was not included but that did not deter anyone from ordering wine.

"Good," said Joe. "Cameriere (Waiter), bring me a bottle of *vino rosso* (red wine). Now, let us make a toast to celebrate the beginning of our tour."

Everybody got a glass of wine and shouted "Salute!"

"Cameriere, could I have another bottle of water?" Betty asked.

"With or without gas?" replied the waiter.

"With gas? What is that? I never heard of that. You put gasoline in the water?" she wondered.

"Water with gas is a sparkling water. It tastes almost like Sprite," explained the waiter.

"Cameriere, bring me another bottle of red wine and make it without gas!" said Mike with a playful laugh.

A few people had a generous refill of spaghetti when the waiter came back with a large platter.

That night for main course, we had veal cutlet with golden roasted potatoes and asparagus. For dessert, they placed on each table a large basket with fresh grapes, pears, figs, and apples. Some people wanted coffee, but they were told in Italy they didn't serve coffee with dinner (they drink wine!). However, they served plenty of coffee for breakfast. During any other time, people could get coffee at the hotel bar. In Italy "bar" means "coffee shop".

"Oh, never mind," said Tony. "Just bring me a glass of that delicious liquor Amaroto de Sorano."

"Do you mean Amaretto di Saronno?" replied the waiter.

"Oh, yes, yes. That's it! Sorry about my broken Italian!"

"Cameriere, make it four glasses," added Joe.

After dinner, most people sat on the dimly lit terrace in front of the restaurant. They enjoyed the view of *Stresa by Night*, about 1500 feet down below. Then, one by one, they retreated to their rooms for a good night sleep.

"So far, so good," Angela told me.

I wished everyone "Buona Notte!" (Good night), and asked Alberto to wake us at 6:30 in the morning. Within a few minutes, we were all soundly sleeping.

Lago Maggiore: Isola Bella

CHAPTER 4

MILAN, THE PRIDE OF NORTH ITALY

The next morning in the picturesque Alpine village of Nebbiuno a rooster from a nearby farm woke up the neighborhood. Before long, a few sheep joined the concert. Some of us did not pay attention, but many woke up to that concert. Then, at 6:30 a.m., everybody's phone chimed: "Ring, ring, ring". I rolled out of bed, opened the window, looked outside, and enjoyed a spectacular view: the rising sun peeked between the mountains. It was a beautiful and inspiring scene to begin our day. Next to my room, I heard a man singing, "*O Sole Mio…!*"

Mary came to the breakfast room chanting, "It is such a pretty day. Look at the bright sunshine!"

Everybody was in a festive mood and anxious to continue with the tour. The temperature was perfect, the sky was striking blue, and the sun vibrant. Breakfast was served at 7:30 a.m. It was a generous buffet with a large choice of juicy and tasty food.

"Remo, I see hard-boiled and scrambled eggs, but where is the *bacon?*" Rose asked.

"Dear lady, you are in Italy, not America," I answered. "They don't use bacon here."

"Honey, you forgot, when in Rome do like Romans do," intervened her husband, Luigi.

"Yes, but we are not yet in Rome!" Rose laughed.

I must point out that during a group tour some people display a particular behavior: they are constantly in a cheerful mood; they talk more, walk faster, laugh louder, question everything, and act like care-free teenagers. Unfortunately, sometimes they whine like them too!

While baggage was placed in the bus, I shouted, "Signori e Signore, tutti in carozza!" (Ladies and gentlemen, all aboard). I called the roll and then said: "Buon Giorno! How do you feel after that good night sleep? Are you ready to conquer Italy? Andiamo! (Let us go)."

Antonietta volunteered to say a short prayer every morning. After loading all baggage, Mariano was sweating, but he kept on smiling especially to the ladies.

While we descended the mountain through a scenic and winding road, people gave a last look at Lago Maggiore and made comments about its beauty. The remark that most impressed me was the one made by Paul:

"I have seen many wonderful places, but I have never seen anything like this. The Lago Maggiore, the Alps and these neat little towns. What a wonderful world. I am so happy to be here!"

We entered the freeway and headed for Milan, our destination of the day. The traffic was very heavy. I explained we were in the Region called *Piemonte,* but soon we would return to Lombardia. In fact, as we came out of a tunnel, we drove over Ticino River, which up until 1860 marked the border between the Kingdom of Piemonte and the Grand Duchy of Milan.

I gave a brief, historic account about Italy. "We know about the rise and fall of the great Roman Empire. When the Barbarians invaded this beautiful land, Italy went through a long period of *dark ages.* For more than 1000 years the country was divided into many independent republics, kingdoms and principalities ruled by despotic kings, dukes, barons and warlords. Piemonte, Lombardia, Genoa, Veneto, Ferrara, Florence, Parma, Lucca, Modena, Pisa, Siena, Rome, Amalfi, and Naples were independent states or city-states. Lombardia and its capital Milano were ruled by the powerful Sforza and Visconti families. Finally, in 1870 the King of Piemonte, Victor Emanuel II, through wars and negotiations, united all of Italy into one single country. Actually, the Italian Republic is younger than America!"

"How long is Italy?" Steve inquired.

"From its northernmost point in the Alps to the southernmost tip of the boot it is about eight-hundred-mile long. From the blue Adriatic Sea to the Tyrrhenian Sea on the west it is about one hundred-fifty mile wide."

"Remo, how far is it to Milan? Nature is calling," Luisa said.

"Is it an emergency?"

"No, but don't wait too long."

"Okay. In about twenty minutes we should be there."

I explained that in Italy public restrooms are rare, and if you find one you must pay to use it. The best way is to go to a bar. They might tell you their bathroom is out of order, but, if you ask politely or buy something at a minimum cost, you may use it for free. Again, in Italy "bar" means "coffee shop".

Milan is the second largest city in Italy with a population of about two millions. It is the chief industrial, financial, and commercial center of Italy. It is also the fashion and design capital of Europe; in fact it has been nicknamed *The City of Tailors*. If Rome represents the *Old Italy*, Milan stands for the *New Italy*. However, Milan is not a major tourist attraction, like Venice, Florence, and Rome. When visiting Milan, tourists have in mind only the Duomo, the Galleria, the Scala Opera House, Castle Sforza, and "The Last Supper" by Leonardo da Vinci.

We entered Milan through Viale Certosa and proceeded along the wide and elegant Corso Sempione, lined with luxurious palaces, shops, and restaurants. There were many yellow *streetcars*, like the ones in San Francisco; some were old-fashioned and others super modern.

"Do people live in those buildings?" Marc asked.

"Certainly; as you can see, the ground floor is used for shops and the upper floors for residence."

"Where do they park their cars at night?" John inquired.

"On the street, twenty-four hours per day."

Soon we passed by the *Arch of Peace* built in 1807 to celebrate Napoleon's victories. The *Cimitero Monumentale* (Monumental Cemetery) was next. It contains many artistic tombs for some of the city's most honored citizens.

"Look at that. People here must be very rich to be buried in such elaborate tombs and mausoleums," Ralph remarked.

"That is right," I responded. "In fact, to be buried there, one must meet three conditions: first, be rich; second, be famous, and finally be *dead*!" The bus filled with laughter.

We drove around the large *Arena Civica* (Stadium) where several men were jogging. Finally, we stopped in front of a magnificent fountain with intermittent water jet. We walked to the majestic *Castello Sforzesco,* a medieval masterpiece of architecture built in 1368. I had barely time to tell people to meet at that same spot at 11:00 a.m., when Luisa yelled:

"Remo, the bathroom!"

"Oh, yes, follow me," I quickly responded. To my surprise, I saw the entire group needed relief!

We walked through the two, massive courtyards of the castle. Everything is well-preserved: the immense walls, the draw bridge, the courtyards, the slits, and the large moat. The moat has been drained of its water and now is just a grass-covered ditch. Originally, the castle consisted of many forts enclosed in a great star-shaped fortress with tall ramparts. Today, despite its reduced size, it is still Italy's largest castle. When you enter, you are actually in the medieval times.

"Who lives in this castle?" Susan wanted to know.

"No one lives here now. In the olden times, it was the residence of the *Dukes Sforza* and then the *Visconti*, who ruled in Milan. Today, it houses several museums."

"Could we see the museums?" Rose interrupted.

"No, we don't have time. It takes a good half day, and we have many other interesting sites to see."

"Why do they have all those holes in the walls?" Peter wondered.

"Those are for the pigeons," I said. Since they did not take my explanation, I added, "Actually, those holes held the scaffolds when they built the castle. They are still used for repairs."

"Oh, look at those enormous stone balls! What are they?" Betty marveled.

"Betty, those are *bocce balls*!" (lawn bowling), Paul responded.

I laughed and explained those were real cannon balls, used many centuries ago.

"How old is this castle?" Mary asked.

"About 700 years old."

"What did he say?" shouted Sandra, next to me. Linda distracted her.

"Look at all those wild cats in the moat," said Karen, pointing out several cats lounging by the cannon balls.

I announced, "Now you have forty-five minutes free time for pictures and browsing around."

At 11:00 a.m., everyone was back by said magnificent fountain. I took the roll-call and then we walked along Via Dante. People followed my red carnation like boy scouts follow their leader.

"Who is that guy on the horse up there?" Mario inquired, as we walked by a huge statue.

"That is the statue of *Giuseppe Garibaldi,* the great general who was instrumental in uniting Italy into one country."

"Oh, yes, yes. My nonno (grandfather) told me about him."

We proceeded into the charming and luxurious *Via Dante* connecting two of the most important areas of the city. Elegant palaces, expensive shops, and sidewalk cafés border the street crowded with people drinking coffee, eating snacks, or enjoying a *gelato* (ice cream). Via Dante is reserved for pedestrians only. Occasionally, Milanesi use the entire street for artistic displays. The day we walked through it, they celebrated the "Settimana della Vacca" (The Week of the Cow). They had at least fifty plastic cows lined up in the middle of the street. Each cow had a different color and a different design.

At the end of Via Dante we entered *Piazza Duomo* with a large crowd of busy people going in all directions, but what caught our immediate attention was the view of the majestic Gothic styled *Duomo*. It is the fifth largest and one of the most beautiful cathedrals in the world. It is also the center, symbol and pride of Milan. The Duomo is dedicated to the Virgin Mary.

Construction of the Duomo began in 1386 and it took about 500 years to complete! It can hold 40,000 people at one time. Remarkably, it is entirely made of marble, even the walls, the floor and the roof. The elaborate designs are simply outstanding: it is decorated with 96 gargoyles, 135 spires, and 3159 marble statues of which 2245 are located on the outside. Imagine: if those statues were placed on top of each other, they would reach a height of about 3.3 miles! We can guess how many artists were involved in sculpting all those beautiful statues and how many years of planning, building, sculpting, chiseling, polishing, and measuring it took to build the Duomo! How much did it cost? We don't know, but the Milanesi definitely put their money where their faith was.

The entrance to the Duomo is free, but visitors must go through a security check and need to be appropriately dressed: no shorts or strapless tops. The interior of the Duomo is astonishing. When entering, one finds it rather dark with some light coming through the glass windows, but slowly, as the eyes adjust, one discovers the wonders of the church. High above the main altar hangs a red light indicating a niche that contains a "Holy Nail", believed to be one of the nails with which Jesus was crucified. It was brought from the Holy Land by St. Helen, mother of the emperor, Constantine.

Many tourists take a fascinating trip to the *Rooftop* of the Duomo. The entrance is located outside, on the left side of the Duomo. To get up there, one must climb 250 steps or take the elevator. Once on the rooftop, people walk through a phantasmagorical forest of 135 marble spires, flying buttresses, pinnacles, ornate steeples, sculptures, tracery, statues, and gargoyles. It is amazing, fantastic, and stunning! The view from up there is spectacular. One can see the entire city of Milan and the snowy peaks of the Alps.

Looking further up on the highest spire, one can see a seventeen-foot-tall statue of the *Madonnina* (the Little Madonna). It is made of copper and coated with 3900 pieces of golden leaves. The statue was placed up there in 1774, at a height of 350 feet. A popular song dedicated to the Madonnina became the official city's anthem. The song goes: "O Mia Bella Madonnina…" (Oh my Beautiful Little Madonna…)

The bustling Piazza Duomo, right in front of the church, is the heart of Milan. In the middle stands the colossal statue of King Vittorio Emnauele II. It seems to be keeping a watchful eye over the Duomo and the crowd of people and pigeons.

Milan: Duomo

Walking under a huge triumphal arch, on the left of the Duomo, we entered the prestigious and bustling *Galleria*. Milanesi call it *Il Salotto di Milano* (Milan's Living Room) because of its numerous shops and importance as a common meeting and dining place for the Milanesi.

That Galleria is the first, and most beautiful, shopping mall of modern times. It was designed by the architect Giuseppe Mengoni and inaugurated in 1867 and consists of four impressive palaces enclosed by a glass dome and decorated with lovely paintings in each corner. The floor has many artistic designs made with marble and mosaics. Inside the Galleria, one finds elegant restaurants, cafés, bars, and luxurious boutiques selling haute couture, jewelry, books, and paintings. Yes, it is the favorite place for businessmen and women, artists, opera singers, fashion models, and tourists. It is also perfect for window-shopping, strolling, and admiring the elegance of Milanesi passing by.

People are welcome to enter the Galleria, but a wide net under the entrance arch keeps pigeons away. However, small birds do venture inside and cautiously flutter about the cafés and clean the floor of crumbs.

Unexpectedly, something odd distracted my amazed visitors in the Galleria. Right in the center, on the floor, there is a mosaic picture of a dancing *bull*. Tourists stand in line to *crush the bull's balls*! You place your heel over the balls, spin around in a circle three times without tripping and make a wish. Why? They say your wish will come true. Poor bull, his tile balls become so worn out that the tiles must be replaced quite often!

"John, get in there right now and crush those things!" yelled John's wife.

One by one, laughing and joking, everybody wanted a picture while abusing that poor bull.

Walking eastward, we exited the Galleria and arrived to *Piazza della Scala*. The statue of Leonardo da Vinci greeted us and pointed out the world's most prestigious opera house, *La Scala*. That is where over 600 different opera singers, composers, and actors performed and gained fame: just think of Giuseppe Verdi, Donizetti, Puccini, Bellini, Rossini, and Maria Callas. Today, classical ballets, operas, operettas, and concerts are presented in this opera house. It is the dream of every musician to visit this place.

Constructed in 1776 by Giuseppe Piermarini, La Scala can accommodate more than 2000 spectators. The outside of the building has nothing special, but the interior is spectacular: it has six rows of decorated loggias, fluted columns, red velvet boxes, silk and gilded stuccos, gleaming mirrors, and a huge chandelier with 365 lamps hanging in the center. If you stand at the entrance door on a performance day, you will see people fashionably dressed. If you go inside, watch the performance, and listen to the classical music, you will be transported into the realm of fantasy and dream of being a prince or princess.

"Can we stay for a performance?" Joan implored.

"Sadly, no, we cannot. You are lucky if you can get tickets a month ahead of a performance. However, you can have a picture taken while you sing in front of La Scala and tell your friends back home you were a *singer* at La Scala!"

We strolled back through the Galleria and stopped in front of the Duomo. It was 12:30 p.m. I explained in the center of Milan there are many interesting streets, but my favorite one is *Corso Vittorio Emanuele*, behind the left side of the Duomo. It is a beautiful pedestrian avenue where women walk with grace and elegance and men have suits and neckties. Along the Corso, one can see mimes, street musicians, glamorous boutiques, and sidewalk cafés. When we visited the Corso, there was an exhibit of large posters showing some of the most picturesque places of the Italian Peninsula.

"Where is a good place to eat?" Tony enquired.

"Tony, I don't recommend any specific restaurant because there are so many. You decide which one is good for your taste and wallet. However, I suggest before you sit down to eat, you look at what people are eating and decide if it is appealing to you. Then, make sure you check the cost on the menu." I added for fun, "There are at least three McDonalds in this area."

"Come on. I did not come to Italy to eat at McDonalds!" Tony objected.

My group had two hours of free time. At 2:30 p.m., everybody was back in front of the Duomo. From there we walked to the *Church of Santa Maria delle Grazie* and went to see the famous *Cenacolo*, known as "The Last Supper", painted by Leonardo da Vinci in 1494. It is housed in the refectory of a Dominican convent, adjacent to the church. The famous masterpiece depicts the consternation that occurred among the apostles at the moment Jesus said one of them would betray him.

Years ago, anyone could stand in line, buy a ticket, and see Leonardo's work, but, as the crowd of visitors grew out of proportion, one needed to make reservations a couple of months in advance. We had our reservation, therefore, at 3:00 p.m., we were lead into said refectory. Tourists were admitted by small groups of twenty-five and allowed only fifteen minutes to view the painting. The rule of complete silence and no pictures was strictly enforced. We rented an audio guide to learn about the painting.

"The Last Supper" is indeed the famous painting people from all the over the world go to admire. However, on the opposite wall of Leonardo's masterpiece visitors can see another lovely mural, the *Crucifixion* by Donato Montorfano. It is bigger and perhaps more impressive than Leonardo's work, but people have never heard of it and barely notice it on their way out. Well, the name of the artist makes the difference: who ever heard of Donato Montorfano?

The visit to "The Last Supper" concluded our stay in that glorious city. On our way out, I asked, "How do you like Milano?"

"Fantastic!" was the unanimous answer.

People wished to spend a few more days in Milan, but we were on a tour of Italy not Milan. "Our tour is like a photo album," I explained, "every day you see something new, something beautiful. More wonderful surprises are in-store for you during this tour."

We took the freeway headed for *Venezia* (Venice), which also connects north Italy to the surrounding countries. The traffic was heavy with cars and large trucks. There were also trucks and busses from Austria, France, Yugoslavia, Switzerland, Greece, Hungary, Germany, Albania, Rumania, and Russia.

I explained, "If you see the letter 'I' on the left side of the license plate, that means the vehicle is from Italy. The letter 'D' means Germany, 'F' is France, 'E' stands for Spain, 'A' is Austria, 'CH' means Switzerland, etc." I continued, "The numbers posted along the road are not miles, but kilometers. It takes 1.6 kilometer to have one mile. Look at that sign; it says, 'Venice is 140 kilometers away.' How many miles is that?"

Milan: stepping on the Bull's Balls

I heard someone answer about eighty-five miles. Soon, I noticed almost everybody was falling asleep, so I kept quiet as we bypassed the city of Bergamo and Brescia.

Around 5:30 p.m., I picked up the microphone and whispered, "Wake up, wake up." We took a coffee and bathroom break in a nice *Autogrill*, built above the freeway. I instructed, "If you want a drink at the bar, first tell the cashier what you want, pay, get the ticket, and then show it to the waiter, and you will be served. Waiters handle no money."

I also explained usually at the entrance of the restroom is a cleaning woman and a dish on a table; she appreciates a small tip. While all men had already left, the line in front of the women's bathroom was still long.

"I wish I were a man and could get in and out quickly," Sandra whined.

After returning to the bus, Mary wanted an explanation about something that puzzled her. "Remo, next to the toilet bowl in my hotel room there was another smaller bowl. What is it? I never saw anything like it before."

"That is called *bidet* and you should use it to wash your feet," I teased.

"And something else," added Peter.

"Like what?" Mary wanted to know.

"To wash your *culo* (butt)." Angela laughed.

"And something else," insisted Peter.

"Like what?" Mary replied, impatiently.

"To wash the culo's cousin!" Peter explained.

On the road again, we passed by *Verona*, the city known for its well-preserved *Roman Amphitheater* and the Castle of *Romeo and Juliet*. Soon, people marveled:

"Look, vineyards everywhere! The vines are loaded with grapes!"

It was mid-September and farmers were getting ready to harvest them.

"At what time is dinner?" Ralph asked.

"I never know. I must ask at the hotel. If they have other groups before us, they go by the rule, 'first come, first served.' Anyway, dinner is never served before 7:30 p.m."

When we arrived in Padua, people were rather tired. The modern *Hotel Galileo* was our host for the next two days. Dinner was at 7:30 p.m. We were served delicious homemade pasta, salad, tasty pork chops, roasted potatoes, and a large slice of cake. Wine was included. After that, my gentle thirty-five diners left the restaurant, jolly, and tipsy. Some of them sat in the bar, some walked outside, and others retreated to their bedroom. Buona Notte!

CHAPTER 5

VENICE, A FAIRY-TALE CITY

They say the city of *Venice* was named after *Venus*, the goddess of love and beauty. The goddess was born from the sea and, likewise, Venice was born from the sea and certainly is a city that inspires love and beauty.

Venice, Florence, and Rome are the three Italian cities all tourists long to see. Florence attracts visitors with its perfect blend of art and culture and Rome because of its historic and religious significance. But what is so special about Venice that fascinates all visitors? What is there about Venice that attracts more than twenty million tourists a year?

Well, people of all ages enjoy fairytales and Venice seems to be a fairy-tale city rising from the sea. It appears like a dream, a mirage springing from the waters of the lagoon. Walking through its streets is like stepping into a fantasy world, into a magic vision; one feels like being in Wonderland. But Venice is not a fairy-tale, it is a reality; it is unique, beautiful, and romantic; Venice enchants and fascinates and has the power to make dreams come true. This city inspires countless poets, artists, musicians, intellectuals, and travelers.

Lord Byron wrote: "I loved her (Venice) from my boyhood; to me she was a fairy-city of the heart, rising from the sea." Numerous places around the world are named after Venice: there is the Venice of Holland, of Quebec, of Thailand, and the Venice of Florida, but there is only one true Venice (Venezia), the city with undeniable presence. That romantic city is our destination today.

Early in the morning of Day Four of our tour, I entered the breakfast room and found my thirty-five vacationers very eager to start their new adventure. Yes, Milan was a delightful surprise, but Venice was in everybody's hearts. I was greeted enthusiastically:

"Buon Giorno, Remo. What a great breakfast! They have everything, *even bacon*!"

"Have any of you ever been to Venezia?" I asked.

"Yes, in my dreams!" responded Paul

"I had a taste of it when I saw the Venetian Palace in Las Vegas," added Ralph.

"Well, rejoice, because today your dream will come true." Without hesitation, I sang the Gondolier's song, "Gon…do…la, Gon…do…la, Gon… do…li." I had not finished singing when Marc started:

"Venus! Oh, Venus! Make my dream come true!" We thought Frankie Avalon had joined our group.

At 8:30 a.m., everybody was on the bus, smiling and greeting each other. It was another sunny day. Mariano asked if I noticed he had washed all windows on the bus. He took pride in his work and kept the bus clean, inside and out. The prayer was said and we rolled towards *Venezia*, known as *The Queen of the Adriatic, The Serenissima, The Romantic City by excellence, The Floating City*, and *The City of Canals*.

In route, I gave the following account about the origins of that magic city: "When we look at Venice, we wonder why they built it entirely on the water. Couldn't they build it on solid ground? Were the Venetians crazy or from outer space? No, they were neither crazy nor from outer space. Venice was born out of a struggle for survival. Some 1500 years ago, when the Roman Empire fell apart, the *barbarian* hordes swept over north Italy like a hurricane, burning and destroying everything. Imagine: the barbarian leader of the Huns, *Attila*, known as *The Scourge of God*, used to brag: 'Where my horse steps there will be no more grass growing.' Facing an onslaught, people from the mainland found refuge on the 117 offshore marshy lagoons and inhabited islets near the coast. The Barbarians were good horsemen but bad boatmen, therefore those refugees were safe there. They squatted on that miserable land, sank numerous pilings in the mud and built their dwelling on them; they channeled water into many canals, constructed bridges and linked together the islets. That miserable beginning later became the glorious Venice."

"We know the children's story of the *Three Little Pigs*. First, they built their house of straw, then a house of sticks, and finally a house of bricks. Similarly, the refugees lived in tents and piled-dwellings, but, in time, they forgot their land-based origins and became used to living on water, and slowly their living conditions improved. There was no more fear of the Barbarians: the invaders and the invaded melted into one people. Those refugees became expert in harvesting salt and fish, which they sold on the mainland. In the 8th century, Venice developed into a *republic* ruled by a *Doge* (from Latin *Dux* = Leader) and called itself *Serenissima* (The Most Serene). To glorify its achievements, in 828 Venice brought the remains of the *Apostle St. Mark* from Egypt, declared him *patron saint*, and built for him an elaborate basilica. Actually, the Venetian merchants stole the relics of the saint and, to pass them through the Muslim customs, they cleverly hid the relics under a layer of pork. Muslims consider the pig unclean and detest touching pork meat."

"Over the next centuries, the Venetians became expert seamen, grew into a great maritime power, traveled everywhere; (we know Marco Polo went even further, to China), established a very prosperous commerce with countries in the Middle East, and conquered the world's business. They had the monopoly on transporting Eastern goods, especially silk, grain, and spices, to Venice, which then were sold to other European countries. By the year 1300, the city became the wealthiest and most powerful city of Europe. At the peak of its power, the city had a population of 400,000; of those 36,000 were sailors and operated a strong fleet of 3,300 ships! The city was also embellished with splendid palaces, 400 canals, 409 foot bridges, 3000 alleyways,

107 artistic churches, and numerous picturesque piazzas. True, during the Middle Ages, while the rest of the world was laying into a cultural lethargy, numerous painters, architects, sculptors, engravers, and decorators made Venice an extraordinarily beautiful city, a living museum. That *City of Canals* became a city of pageantry, a city of splendors, and a very busy money market. What an incredible achievement from the miserable origins in the unhealthy marshes!"

"The Venetian Republic lasted for more than a thousand years. After such a glorious history and independence, in 1866 it volunteered to become united to the Italian kingdom. By losing its political independence, Venezia did not lose its cultural uniqueness; rather, it became one of the most interesting vacation destinations in the world. Yes, today the Venetians live of their past and they make full use of it."

By the time I finished talking about Venezia, our bus approached the two-mile-long *Ponte della Liberta'* (Freedom Bridge), which connects mainland with the outskirts of the city. That bridge was opened in 1933. Before that time, boats were the only means of transportation between Venice and the mainland.

Excitement was on everybody's face when we reached the parking lot of the *Tronchetto*, an artificial island. I purchased tickets for the *Vaporetto*, a large water-bus, and then I shouted: "Andiamo!" (Let us go). We entered a covered platform mostly packed with tourists.

A few minutes later, an impatient lady in my group whined, "When will this boat leave? What are we waiting for?"

A smart aleck (actually, a Calabrese tour guide) replied, "Lady, this is not the boat. This is the waiting room. The boat is on the way."

Within minutes we boarded a Vaporetto and navigated over the famous *Canal Grande*. Our Venetian dream began to unfold. Canal Grande, shaped like an "S", snakes through the heart of Venice; it is the city's main waterway; it is three-mile-long, 150 feet wide and 16 ft. deep. The canal is lined on both sides with more than 170 color-washed splendid palaces rising from the rippling waters. The palaces are not all the same style and architecture; some are Gothic, others Moorish, Renaissance, or Rococo. Most of them date from the 13th to the 18th century and demonstrate the welfare and art created by the Republic of Venice. To mention a few: Palazzo Vendramin (the composer Richard Wagner died in there), Palazzo Pesaro, Ca' D'Oro (its façade was once completely covered with golden leaves), Palazzo Manin, Palazzo Rezzonico, Ca' Grande, etc. Those, and many more palaces, were former residence of the Venetian nobility. Each palace is a priceless masterpiece of architecture. In front of a few, one can find elegant restaurants built on a deck right above the water and the entrance directly from the waterway. In front of others, we noticed *poles* sticking out of the water; they marked with white and blue or white and red stripes and looked just like the sign in front of the American barber shops; those poles mark the parking lots for moored gondolas. The traffic on Canal Grande was heavy with water-buses, barges, water-taxis, police boats, fireboats, ambulances, garbage barges, and gondolas. Here and there, people could be seen walking or sitting along the waterfront; some tourists had their feet dangling in the water.

My people became exhilarated. Immediately, many took pictures and bombarded me with questions:

"How deep is this canal?"

"How old is that building?"

"Do they have fish in the canal?"

"How did they build those magnificent palaces?"

"How do they get their drinking water?"

"How is their sewer system?"

"Did anyone ever fall in the water?"

"Are there any paved streets?"

Angela and Susan daydreamed when they saw a romantic couple in a gondola gliding through the water.

Mario asked, "Remo, I heard they have a Casino in Venice. Where is it?"

"Yes, there is a Casino. Why do you want to go there?"

"To have fun; what else?"

"My friend, you are confused. A casino is a whorehouse. Maybe you mean a casino' with an accent on the 'O'."

"Well, what is the difference? You have fun in both places!" Mario laughed.

Our Vaporetto passed by the church of Santa Lucia, where her mortal remains are venerated. Then we passed under Rialto Bridge; people waved at us from up there. I had instructed my people to leave the boat only in front of St. Mark's Square. When our Vaporetto made a stop by Rialto Bridge, a lot of people disembarked, including Vincent. We yelled at him. He raised his hands in surprise, but he did not seem concerned. That was his fourth tour with me and he knew where to find us.

Finally, we disembarked at Pontile San Marco. There we found many tourists browsing by souvenir stands; a few artists captured the Venetian beauty on their canvases.

When we arrived at *Piazzetta St. Mark,* I raised my r*ed carnation,* pulled the group in a corner and shouted, "Come closer!"

Mary put her arm around me and said, "Closer than this?"

"Hear me, hear me," I said, "now we begin our *orientation tour.* Keep an eye on the group and my carnation. You will see shops everywhere; it will be hard to resist, but please, do not stop. You will have plenty of free time for shopping after this walking tour. If you get lost, go to the Bell Tower in St. Mark's Square, and wait there. If you get totally lost, you should take a water-taxi, a train, and another taxi to return to your hotel. That could cost you about $200. Don't make that expensive mistake! Do you know the name of your hotel? Okay? Andiamo!" I believe I alarmed them enough to keep their attention during the entire walking tour! It was 10:45 a.m.

In the Piazzetta, I pointed out two tall granite columns erected in 1172 as official gateway to the city. The column on the left is surmounted by the statue of St. Theodore killing a dragon that fed on humans and the column on the right holds a winged lion, symbol of St. Mark and of the Venetian Republic. A pigeon was basking on the lion's tail and another one on Theodore's head.

An enormous, white palace in the Piazzetta caught everybody's attention. Its façade has a marvelous open portico with Gothic arches decorated with historic and biblical scenes. An impressive row of wonderful interwoven arches surmounts the portico. The upper floor looks like a pale pink dress, crowned with golden battlements. Looking at that gorgeous palace, at first glance one has the impression it rises from the waters of the lagoon inexplicably, by magic, like the goddess, Venus, who rose from the sea.

"That is the *Doge's Palace,* the residence of the supreme authority in Venice since the 9th century," I explained. "It is more than a thousand years old. Imagine: when America was discovered, the Doge's Palace was already five hundred years old. I recommend, during your free time today, you visit it. In there, you will find artistic courtyards, large halls, marble fireplaces, plaster relief ceilings, paintings, sculptures, sumptuous decorations, and incredible works of art. See the stunning Hall of the Great Council, which can hold 2500 people. See its ceiling covered with gold and the walls with enormous frescoes. Don't miss seeing the *Paradise,* by Tintoretto, the largest painting in the world; it measures 60 x 22 ft. The most famous artists of the 16th century, mainly Veronese, Tintoretto, Tiepolo, Bellini, Tiziani, and Palma worked to embellish that Doge's Palace."

"Remo, what is that color-washed church across the canal?" Betty asked.

"That is the church of *St. George* on the St. George Island. Look at the very spot where Luisa is standing; in olden times hundreds of public executions, especially for gays, took place right there."

Luisa jumped back with terror, and screamed, "Oh, my God!"

Next, we moved over *Ponte della Paglia* (Straw Bridge) and I pointed out, suspended high above a narrow canal, a small whitish enclosed bridge made of white limestone. The two tiny windows in the middle have stone bars. That bridge connects the prison cells on the right to the courtroom in the Doge's Palace on the left. "That is the famous *Bridge of Sighs,* designed by Antonio Contino in 1602. The

Venetians claim if at sunset you ride a gondola under that bridge and kiss your partner, your love will be forever." Supposedly, the *sighs* come from lovers who are overwhelmed by the romance of the entire scene. Oh, yes, that bridge has seen thousands of couples sighing, dreaming, and kissing passionately!

I heard Susan sigh: "Oh, Carlo, my sweetheart, where are you?"

The sad reality is that in olden times, when the convicts were taken from the courtroom to their terrible cells, or their executioner, they could stop a few seconds by those two tiny windows, catch a last glimpse of Venice, and *sigh* for their lost freedom or life. "Good-bye, cruel world. I am innocent! Mamma, I didn't do it!"

> "I stood in Venice, on the Bridge of Sighs,
> a palace and a prison on each hand."
>
> George Byron

Bridge of Sighs

Yes, when prisoners walked over that bridge, they ceased to exist, they fell into oblivion; there was no chance of escaping. Among the unfortunate residents of that jail was the famous womanizer, *Giacomo Casanova*, arrested in 1775. Unbelievable, but true, he was the only one able to escape. They say he did it with the help of his secret lover, the warden's daughter. Today, visitors can still see that terrible prison. In fact, the same ticket that gives access to the Doge's Palace also gives access to those awful jail cells.

While we slowly walked to St. Mark's Square, an enormous cruise ship slid silently in the Canale della Giudecca. Hundreds of people waved from the top deck.

We strolled into the amazing *St. Mark's Square*, the political, civil, religious, and artistic center of Venice; it is also its symbol and pride. The Square is rectangular and bordered by two long palaces with elegant floors of loggias. An open portico runs on the ground floor of the palaces and three rows of beautiful superimposed Romanesque arches adorn the upper floors. The Square is a meeting place for the Venetians and the tourists alike. Visitors say it is the most beautiful square in the world. Napoleon called it "The finest drawing room in Europe."

"Those palaces are the *Procuratie*," I explained. "Formerly, they were offices of the glorious Venetian Republic. Today, they are used as shops and restaurants at the ground level and museums in the upper floors. On both sides of the Square, you can see an open-air café with an orchestra playing soft music. It is pleasant to relax there with a drink, but expect to pay a very high price."

Two couples were romantically dancing. Tony and Karen joined them.

In the center of the Square, when I saw many children chasing pigeons, I wished I could do the same, but I preferred to buy a small bag of birdseed. Immediately, a swarm of hungry *pigeons* landed around me; some climbed on my head, arms, and hands. Flapping their wings and dropping a few feathers, they refused to budge from my feet. I gave the rest of the food to Sandra and Paul near me and said: "Remember, if a pigeon drops something on you, soon you will receive some good news." People laughed at my explanation, but they had fun being photographed among the whirling cloud of pigeons.

Yes, the Procuratie form an extraordinary architectonic complex, but the jewel of St. Mark's Square is the more than thousand-year-old *St. Mark's Basilica,* known as *The Church of Gold.* It looks like a mirage with a harmonious combination of arches, onion domes, glitter of mosaics and elegant decorations and minarets soaring upwards into the azure sky. It is a conglomeration of Romanesque, Byzantine, Islamic, Moorish, Gothic, and Renaissance architecture. The Basilica, in the form of a Greek cross, was built to house the mortal remains of St. Mark the Evangelist, patron saint of the city.

Standing in front of the basilica, I pointed out the lovely white and pink marble mosaics depicting religious scenes in the façade. We admired "The Last Supper", "The Resurrection", "The Ascension", "The Deposition from the Cross", "The Prophets", and "Noah and the Stealing of St. Mark's Body".

On the loggia, above the main portal, we saw the marvelous four *Bronze Horses* dating from the 4th century BC. Those stood for centuries over the main entrance of the Hippodrome in Constantinople. The Crusaders plundered and took them to Venice. Imagine: to make them fit into the ship, their heads were cut off, and then reattached in Venice. Collars now hide the cuts. Those horses are copies; the originals are in a museum.

We did not enter the Basilica. I suggested people visit it during their free time. "The interior of the church gives an idea of what once was the splendor of Venice," I explained. "You will be dazzled by the precious and brilliant mosaics, gilt and golden inlays that cover the walls, ceilings, and domes. Even the floor is made of multicolored marble mosaics tessellated in geometric patterns. The upper level of the interior is completely covered with bright golden mosaics. Look at the mosaics representing "Christ Pantocreator", "The Ascension", "The Pentecost", "The Apocalypse", "The Slaughter of Innocents", "Joseph Taken to Egypt", "Joseph and His Brothers", "The Dance of Salome", and many more biblical scenes. Look at the gleaming, massive piers and lofty cupolas which rise ninety-three feet high. Visit the Tomb of St. Mark in the crypt and don't miss seeing the *Pala d'Oro* (Golden Cloth), a very rich altar covered with more than 3000 precious stones and enamel icons."

By St. Mark's Basilica stands the 325-foot-tall, red brick *Campanile* (Bell Tower), originally built as a lighthouse in the lagoon. An elevator quickly takes people to the top. From there, one can enjoy beautiful views of Venice, the lagoon, and the Alps in the distance.

"It is eleven o'clock. Look at that magnificent astronomical *Clock Tower*. Its enameled and gilded facade indicates the time, the changing of seasons, phases of the moon, and the movement of the sun. Every hour on the hour, the two bronze statues of Moors on top of the tower strike that huge bell with their heavy hammer." I had barely finished saying this when the Moor on the right moved and, "Bam! Bam!" it hit that bell eleven times. A few seconds later, the Moor on the left did the same. Those punctual two Moors have been faithfully performing their duty for more than 500 years, day and night, rain, or shine.

Venice: St. Mark's Basilica

"Hear me!" I demanded. "At five o'clock, we will regroup by this Bell Tower. Okay?"

"Sir, is this the end of the tour?" Sandra asked.

"When do we go on the gondola? Will we have time for that?" Joe enquired, quite concerned.

"Have a little more patience," I responded. "Our walking tour will end at Rialto Bridge. There, I will show where you can take the gondola."

"Is it true Venice gets flooded sometimes?" Ann asked.

"Yes, they have *acqua alta* (high water), especially during the hightide and heavy rains in November and December. When that happens, people walk on boards, but usually the water recedes in the early afternoon."

Venice grew out of the marshy lagoons where the refugees, escaping the barbaric tribes, found safety; they lived in stilt houses on the tiny islets. Space was very limited and with the population increase, they had to use every inch of land for housing. The water-canals were their streets for all purposes, even to enter the residences. In the later centuries brick and stone construction replaced the primitive sheds and some back alleys were converted into pedestrian streets and piazzas. The houses, canals, bridges, buildings, piazzas, and streets we admire today were all built from the 12th to the 15th centuries. Today, they look like a picturesque maze made of old and winding streets.

I wanted to give my visitors a little touch of the Venetians' daily tasks in the back alleys, away from the crowd of foreign tourists. We walked around some of the oldest and winding streets and soon we found ourselves in one of the many small and quaint squares, called "campo" (field). In the center of the campo there was a covered well, two metal benches and a small table by it. In the corners of the campo, there were a few green trees, some thick shrubs, several large pots of flowers, and a small grocery store. The locals use the campos as a place to meet their friends and neighbors and to pass some time of the day over a drink at a café. In fact, we saw five elderly men sitting on benches and playing cards. Two small cafés with outside tables had a few tourists savoring a cappuccino and pizza. The smell of some pasta sauce from an open door made all of us hungry, therefore, we sat in a café and relaxed for a moment.

While enjoying our snack and drinks, we had the pleasure of watching the residents go about their daily life. A few children played ball in a corner of the campo. From an open window, we heard a soprano rehears *La Traviata*. From another window came the sound of someone practicing guitar. An old woman with a basket of fresh vegetables passed right in front of our table. A young priest with a shining, leather briefcase smiled at us and hastened to get to a small bridge over a tiny canal. We could smell the laundry hanging out to dry. A few birds walked under our table searching for crumbs.

Mario saw a pretty brunette staring at us while watering flowers in her window. He waved at her; she waved back and blew a kiss at him. Oh, believe it, for a moment Mario seemed transported in the realm of dreams! We all loved our stop at the campo, and then we continued wandering through more back alleys. My visitors took a picture of anything that seemed unique and beautiful.

Yes, many Venetian streets are paved with water, but those are for boats, of course. The pedestrian streets are paved with flat cobblestones. Some streets are only ten feet wide, others are much narrower. Since most restaurants have tables out into the streets, passers-by must walk among diners to get to their destination. The buildings on the ground floor along the major streets are used for shops, cafés, and restaurants. The floors above the ground level are private residences. Venetians access their residence through a narrow door leading to a steep staircase. The top of most doors is arched or pointed; some have a sculptured roundel representing a lamb, a winged lion, a family crest, angels, or other decorations.

The Venetian piled up housings need light and air, therefore, most buildings have many windows and balconies. Those are high and adorned with verdant creepers, pots of geraniums on windowsills and birdcages on the balcony. Dark green shutters and colorful awnings, flowers, and wrought iron-work add luster to those charming windows. The exterior walls of the buildings are covered with stucco of assorted colors, mostly white, peach or red. Here and there, a plaster peeling off the walls shows eroded and old red bricks underneath.

All roofs are covered with red tiles; some have elaborated and comfortable *altanas,* which are small terraces decorated with flowers, green ferns, tables, and chairs. The altanas are used to hang up clothes to dry or hold a small garden of geraniums and other pot plants; they give also the opportunity to relax under the sun, to take fresh air and have a drink with friends. To prevent fire, all chimneys rise tall above the roofs and have funny shapes.

Narrow, winding *mini-canals* are found at every corner. Some are fifteen feet wide, others are narrower. They are bordered by high and old buildings, intersected by pretty mini-footbridges with artistic stone or metal parapets. Standing on a quiet bridge, one can enjoy watching the *gondoliers,* dressed in traditional striped shirt and wide brimmed hat, dash the oars, row and steer gondolas carrying romantic couples holding hands.

Yes, Venezia has its own Gothic architectural style and own life. It is a unique part of the world. Wandering through the labyrinth of its twisted and intersecting back alleys, strolling in the little squares, seeing the quaint canals and color-washed buildings, and observing life around them is to experience the real magic life of Venezia.

After our adventure in the back alleys, we returned by St. Marc's Square, proceeded slowly under a high archway with said astronomical Clock Tower above it, and walked on *Via Merceria Orologio.* That street, about eight feet wide, constitutes the city's pedestrian *Main Street.* It is the classic shopping district leading to Rialto Bridge. Cozy and fashionable shops with beautiful window displays sell brand name items, Venetian glass, Carnival masks, jewelry, costumes, paintings, and leather goods.

Some of the ladies were tempted to browse in those shops, but I insisted they do that during their free time. I also stated, "Ladies, Florence, not Venice, is your shopping paradise!"

While women lingered by each shop, men were fascinated by the uniqueness of the buildings' architecture.

The crowd on the main Venetian streets is mostly composed of tourists from all over the world; they outnumber the residents. One can hear a different language with every passing couple. Only in restaurants, shops, boutiques, and markets one can hear some Italian being spoken.

"Tom, watch out, there is a car!" Mark yelled.

Tom jumped and looked all around, but there was no car. Venice is a city free of cars. Only a man pushing a cart full of paper boxes was later seen making his way among the crowd. "Attenzione! Attenzione!" (Attention) he kept on shouting. Now and then, we saw a few travelers pull their luggage among the crowd and bump it up and down the steps to cross the bridges. They looked at us and seemed to warn: "Never take a hotel in downtown Venice!"

Via Orologio lead us to the picturesque footbridge *Sottoportego de le Acque*. There were a few people taking pictures of gondolas silently sliding under it. *Trattoria Sempione*, a lovely little hideaway, had an arched window overlooking the canal with water two feet below. Behind pots of geraniums and a hanging green vine, we spotted a romantic couple enjoying food and the view from their table.

"Oh, how I wish my Luigi was here!" Susan sighed.

"Are any fish in these canals?" queried Tony.

"Yes, but rarely. The boat traffic keeps them away," I explained.

"Why do they have so many funny masks for sale?" Joan asked.

"Because a couple of weeks before Ash Wednesday they have the most extravagant carnival in the world. During the festivities, wearing elaborate medieval masks and costumes, revelers of all ages invade the public squares and dance day and night."

Soft music caressed our ears as we passed in front of the Vivaldi Museum on Campo San Salvador. Through another open door, we could hear a singer rehearsing *The Barber of Seville*. On the crowded San Bartolomeo Square, many tourists had lunch in an outside café, under the watchful eyes of Carlo Goldoni's statue, a beloved Venetian playwright.

Finally, we arrived at the beautiful *Rialto Bridge,* a true architectural and engineering achievement of the Renaissance. About 12,000 wooden pilings support this bridge with a single span of 158 feet. The bridge was designed by Antonio da Ponte and completed in 1591. Two inclined ramps lead up to a central portico. On both sides of the bridge, one can find elegant shops with clothes, shoes, jewelry, and various tourist items. From the highest point, we enjoyed a wonderful view of the boat traffic on Canal Grande.

I called everybody's attention: "Ladies and Gentlemen, come closer again. This is the end of our walking tour. Now you are free. Wherever you walk, you will see souvenir shops, restaurants, bars, bridges, canals, gondolas, and tourists. Yes, you should go on a gondola ride;

all tourists do. You can find gondolas right here by this bridge. Ask the gondolier *how much* it costs and *how long* is the ride. A gondola holds up to six people; you can split the cost. Invite the gondolier to serenade you." Furtively looking at some single women in the group, I said, with a smirk, "Remember, that thousands of people found their love while riding the gondola. Who knows?" When you are ready to return, follow the street sign "Per San Marco", or ask the local people. You may also follow the pigeons, since they all go to St. Mark Square!"

A few couples immediately left the group and pursued their own goals. Others were undecided about what to do. They lingered by the bridge and enjoyed the view.

"What happens if I get really lost?" Mary asked.

"Mary, you will not get lost if you follow the advice of singer Tammy Wynette: *Stand by your man.*"

"But, I have no man!"

"Good, then stand by me!" I quickly responded.

"Can I go to *Murano* and buy their glass products?" asked Betty.

"Yes, you can, but you will miss seeing Venice. Besides, you can find the same things here for the same price."

I informed the undecided people I was going to get some fresh figs and grapes at the market around the corner. "You are welcome to stay with me." To my surprise, most of them followed me. We descended to the other side of Rialto Bridge, walked by many souvenir shops, and turned right on San Giacomo Square. There, we found a picturesque outdoor market with many stands selling all kinds of fresh vegetables and fruit. Most stalls had the sign *Non toccare* (Don't touch). The vendors prefer to place the product in cornets of brown paper and to handle it to the clients with a smile and a *Grazie*. Despite the sign, a few old ladies, in traditional dark clothing, felt each apple before putting them in a bag. Even more interesting was what we saw when we heard a fruit vendor yelling:

"Signora, per favore!" (Madam, please!).

Well, it happened that another heavy woman, wearing no bra and an unbuttoned blouse, was leaning on a basket of ripe peaches, sniffing them, and practically touching them with her boobs! A few passing men really enjoyed that scene! Around the corner, we found stalls piled up with many kinds of fish: cuttlefish, sea bass, mussels, clams, scallops, octopus, squid, lobster, and crabs. There were even whole fish with open eyes. We could smell fish and the sea. Some tourists took pictures of the seafood display. A fisherman posed for a picture while cleaning a huge squid.

The market is where the Venetians shop for their daily fresh produce, fruit, vegetables, cheese, meat, and seafood; it is a rich and colorful scene to see. For a tourist, it is the best place to see locals and to get a flavor of the city's life.

"Remo, what do you do during your free time?" Linda wanted to know.

"Ah, that is a secret! You know the song: "Standing on the corner, watching all the girls go by!"

My people laughed and went their way. It was around noon.

What do tourists usually do during their free time in Venice? Most of them relax in some romantic restaurant with the view of a canal, eat pizza or pasta, have a glass of wine, watch gondolas with romantic couples, and smile at tourists passing by. They try to speak some Italian with their waiter. When they receive the bill and cannot figure out why it is so expensive, they console themselves saying:

"What the heck? We are in Venice!"

After lunch they ride a gondola, take pictures of everything, do window and real shopping, and slowly walk back to St. Mark's Square. Other people use their free time to visit the Doge's Palace, the Bridge of Sighs, St. Mark's Basilica, and the Bell Tower. Younger tourists keep walking aimlessly; they stop here and there, take many pictures, and have a snack or a drink at every corner.

At 5:00 p.m., everyone was back to the meeting place. They were exhausted, but very happy. Some men proudly wore the gondolier's straw hat with a large red ribbon. A few ladies wanted everybody to see the glass necklaces and bracelets they had bought.

When the two Moors on the Clock Tower struck said bell five times, I called the roll and we walked back to the boat. We did not go through Canal Grande, but took the Canale della Giudecca. Mariano picked us up at Tronchetto. In the bus, I heard some people say:

"Oh, what a day! I cannot believe I was in Venice!"

"How can I describe it to my friends?"

"I will come back some day."

Betty started to sing: "But I Can't Help Falling in Love" by Elvis. I guess she was referring to Venice.

If the barbarian king Attila could see Venice today he would laugh: "Unga, Punga! I am going to destroy this city too!" Fortunately, he died long ago and the glorious Venice lives today.

At Galileo Hotel, we had an exquisite antipasto, lasagna, steak with fresh peas, and fried egg plant, salad, a mouthwatering slice of cake and all wine we wanted. After dinner, most people in the group stopped at the bar in our hotel. The bartender played dancing music and we had fun.

Having fun on the gondola

CHAPTER 6

PADUA AND A FLORENTINE SQUARE MEAL

On the bright morning of Day Five of our tour, we said *Arrivederci* (Goodbye) to the gentle personnel at Galileo Hotel. While carrying her suitcase to the bus, Linda began to sing: "Oh, What a Beautiful Morning" from *Oklahoma*! Several other ladies immediately joined her. For a moment, I thought I was at La Scala Opera House! Antonietta said the prayer and our tour started again.

Padova (Padua), our home for the past few days, is a city of about 350.000 people. It is located about twenty-five miles west of Venice. It is one of the major cultural and economic centers of northeast Italy. Medieval walls with a moat still surround most of the city. The second oldest European University, founded in 1222, is in that city; Galileo Galilei taught there. The *Cappella (Chapel) degli Scrovegni*, with thirty-eight beautiful biblical paintings by Giotto and the medieval *Palazzo della Ragione*, right in the center of the city, are worthy to see. However, Padova is not a major tourist destination. The vast majority of people visiting that city are not tourists, but pilgrims paying their respect to *St. Anthony*, the patron saint of the city, locally known as "Il Santo" (The Saint).

St. Anthony, a Franciscan monk, spent most of his life preaching the Gospel in Padova. He converted scores of people to Christianity and performed numerous miracles. According to legend, when Anthony began preaching, no one would listen to him, so he went to the river and preached to the fishes that came to listen to him in an enormous number. That miracle got everyone's attention. Among the countless other miracles, St. Anthony reattached severed parts of human bodies and made a newborn baby talk in court to defend the innocence of his own mother. He is mostly portrayed holding the child Jesus or a lily in his arms. He died in Padua in 1231 at the age of thirty-six. Yes, Anthony was a true messenger of God. The moment he died all church bells in the city rang on their own accord. Soon after his death, a large and magnificent Basilica was built in his honor; it is a masterpiece of architecture with a mixture of Romanesque, Byzantine, and Gothic style.

St. Anthony is considered one of the Catholic Church's most popular saints. He is known for helping people find lost objects. For the past 800 years, people from all corners of the world have been going to visit that Basilica as a place of pilgrimage. We too went to pay our respects to the *Santo*.

At the entrance of the Basilica, two security guards made sure we were appropriately dressed and reminded us no pictures were allowed inside. We entered quietly and immediately felt an inner peace. Many pilgrims meditated and prayed, some were on their knees. Their sincere and solemn devotion touched our hearts. Not far, to the left of the nave, we joined a line of people going to touch St. Anthony's tomb. His remains are located behind a simple *greenish marble slab*, on the back of a bright white altar. The most significant religious act all pilgrims do at the saint's tomb is to place their hands on the cool marble slab and to stop for a moment with the soul in deep prayer. Often many devout hands can be seen touching that sacred slab on the same time. It is a moving scene. Some pilgrims also touch the tomb with a rosary, a crucifix, or the picture of a sick or dead loved person. Each of us placed our right hand on the slab and prayed.

Next to the tomb we saw numerous photos and written notes in a large billboard. Those are the "Thank-You" notes from people who received a favor from the saint. The entire chapel is decorated with excellent marble bas-relief sculptures depicting St. Anthony's life, but those decorations are barely noticed by the pilgrims overwhelmed by the spiritual moment.

From the Santo's tomb, we walked slowly to the *Chapel of Relics*. There we saw the *coffin* where he had been buried, a few garments he wore, and a *stone* he used as a pillow. Then, a startling sight, we saw his well-preserved *teeth, tongue, and vocal cords* each incased in a glass box. Proceeding a little further, we stopped at the *Chapel of Blessings* where an old Franciscan monk, mumbling Latin prayers, blessed us, and sprinkled holy water on us.

Adjacent to the Basilica is a large cloister. In there, I pointed out the souvenir shop and the free bathrooms. Finally, I said, "Now you are free. See you at 10:30 in front of the church by the equestrian statue of Gattamelata. By the way, remember there would be no San Antonio, Texas, if there wasn't a San Antonio of Padua."

Pilgrims touching St. Anthony's Tomb

We regrouped at 10:30 a.m. and walked back to our bus. Mariano drove us through the flat and fertile *Po Valley,* Italy's rich agricultural heartland. The entire area is like a manicured garden with every inch of land being accurately cultivated. Italians make use of all land with perfectly planted rows of vegetation and grains. Wheat and corn had already been harvested, but lush vineyards and fruit trees adorned the land. Farmers atop powerful tractors could be seen plowing the fields here and there. We saw a few hunters with hunting dogs. There were many country towns along the road. Quite a different scene from the architecture and crowds we saw in Stresa, Milan, and Venice!

"The beauty of Italy," I said, "is not confined to cities. The picturesque countryside, the mountains, hills, plains, valleys, and rivers also delight the visitors who travel these roads. That is what we are seeing today."

Soon we drove over Italy's longest river, the *Po.* It is wide and it carries an enormous amount of water. During the fall and spring rainy season the Po used to come out of its banks and flood the surrounding area. Today, extensive dykes and levees have been built to correct the problem. As we crossed the Po, we entered the *Emilia-Romagna* region, and then bypassed the city of Ferrara.

John asked, "Is this where they make the Ferraries?"

"No, those cars are made in the nearby city of Modena."

"Modena? That is where they make 'Balsamic Vinegar', right?" Mary said.

"I love cooking with balsamic vinegar!" Angela added.

During my tours, while riding the bus from place to place, I tell jokes and invite others to do the same. It always starts with clean jokes, but then the colorful ones are more popular. Knowing what was coming along the road, I told this short joke:

"There were two chickens walking along a road. A few cars came now and then. At a certain point, the chickens had to cross the road to go home. The first chicken crossed it without hesitation. The second one, upon seeing a car, tried, and tried, but could not make it. Why?"

Nobody had the right answer. Finally, Marc explained, "Because that chicken was a chicken!"

I had barely finished telling that joke, when we passed by a large chicken barn with the picture of a huge rooster on the front wall. "Look," I said, "they have made a monument to the brave chicken that crossed the road!"

Soon after that, the city of *Bologna* appeared on the horizon. Bologna is a city of over half million people. It is called the "Fat, Learned and Turreted City". It is *fat* because they say its food is the best in Italy. It is *learned* because it houses the world's oldest University founded in the 12th century. It is *turreted* because it has many beautiful churches, palaces, and towers. Bologna is also famed for its beautiful porticos covering over twenty miles of city streets. Rain or shine, one can walk in town without umbrella. The shrine of *La Madonna di San Luca* (Our Lady of St. Luke) can be seen on a hill in the outskirts of Bologna. Tradition says the Apostle St. Luke painted the portrait depicting the Virgin Mary, which is kept in that shrine.

We did not make a stop in Bologna, but bypassed it, and then took a break at *Cantagallo Autogrill.* That gave us a chance to stretch our legs and use the bathrooms. "Please don't eat anything," I warned, "because soon you will have a great lunch in Florence."

From Milan to Venice, and from there to Bologna, we had traveled through flat farm land, but after Bologna our bus climbed hills and mountains. Those are the green *Appennini Mountains,* which form the backbone of the Italian peninsula. We bypassed Sasso Marconi, the town where Guglielmo Marconi was born. Then we drove through many tunnels and bridges. Our ears popped because of the high altitude. At the summit, a road sign read: "Toscana". We were in Tuscany, the sunny, and much celebrated, region of Italy. The name of that region alone has the power to arouse a particular feeling of admiration and respect.

We enjoyed the scenery as we drove through more mountains and woodlands. Sandra made us laugh when she said:

"I see no birds in these woods. Aren't any birds in Italy?"

"Sandra," I explained, "in Italy, everybody takes a nap at this time of the day. Even the birds are now having their siesta!" I called Carlo and reassured him, "Stiamo venendo (we are coming). Prepare the best food you have."

In Sesto Fiorentino, a suburb of west Florence, we went to a restaurant called *Da Carlo*, where we enjoyed a traditional Tuscan lunch, a real *square meal*. It is a place where Carlo cooks, his mother Gaetana helps and his wife, Ivana, and daughter, Barbara, serve. As we entered the restaurant, Ivana hugged each of us. The restaurant was cozy and well decorated. The *antipasto* was already on the table: cheese, salami, mozzarella, olives, celery, bread with olive oil, pizza with tomato, and cheese. Bottles of red and white wine were also on the tables.

Two huge bronze statues of naked men adorned the restaurant, copies of the 3000-year-old Greek *Bronzes of Riace*. Several women posed for a picture with them. There were a lot of laughs, pictures, and wine. Soon everyone went wild! Ivana came with a large tray of freshly cooked rigatoni seasoned with the most delicious sauce. We used a lot of cheese. Several people ate two large dishes of rigatoni. We were served all wine we wanted. Next, a quarter of a fried chicken, sausage, green beans, fresh salad, slices of pizza, assorted fresh fruit, cake, ice cream, tiramisu, champagne, coffee, and an after-dinner drink completed our feast.

During our meal, dancing music added much excitement. Many people got up and danced tango, cha-cha, line dance, twist, and rock and roll. We had a real *food festival* and a fantastic time. We loved every minute of it. When we were tipsy and tired of laughing, we thanked, hugged, and bid farewell to our hosts. On the bus, I could hear people say:

"Mamma Mia, I cannot believe I ate that whoooooole thing!"

"It was sooooooooooo good! It was a true square meal!"

"I never had so much fun! I am not going to eat for the next two days!"

"I had a barrel of fun!"

Chef Carlo with us

During the tour, my people expect me to be omniscient. Some women wanted me to tell how Chef Carlo prepared the delicious food we just ate. I had a simple answer: "Ladies, as for food, yes, I am an expert in eating it, not in preparing it!"

After a short ride, we arrived at our deluxe *Hotel Belvedere* in Montecatini. I asked the manager, Elisabetta, to serve us dinner as late as possible because we were not hungry. She graciously agreed to serve us at 8:30 p.m.

Montecatini is a small Tuscan city of about 25,000 people; it is located some thirty miles west of Florence. The city is known for its *health spas,* the best in Italy, which attract many guests and visitors. The water of the spas contains sulfur and sodium carbonate and offers relief to people with arthritis, digestive ailments, and other illness. They also have many facilities such as massage, mud bathing, and beauty treatments.

While sulfur water takes care of the body, people enjoy a *dolce vita* (sweet life) in Montecatini. For that purpose, the town has been embellished with neat tree-lined streets and gorgeous gardens. Luxurious hotels, fashionable restaurants, outside cafés, classy shops, theaters, boutiques, and night clubs combine health with fun and relaxation.

I assumed that, after such an opulent meal at *Da Carlo*, no one would show up for dinner. To my surprise, when I arrived at the dining room, I found out all my thirty-five, happy people were already eating antipasto.

"Mamma Mia, you are eating again?" I asked.

"Hey, we are on a pleasurable vacation. We eat now and diet when we go back home!" Both in quantity and quality we had another great dinner. Red and white wine was included and made us ignore the voices of our stomachs. "Enough is enough!"

After dinner, we walked downtown and passed by a fanciful *merry-go-round* and took a ride. Some passers-by looked at us in a strange way. Well, who said a merry-go-round is only for children? Downtown Montecatini was crowded with visitors and locals, some walking, and others sitting in outside cafés. Using a wireless speaker and an I-phone, Paul played some dancing music on Main Square and most of us danced. To our surprise, within minutes, others surrounded us and all together we had a real *barrel of laughs*.

Pasquale, a local gentleman, sat alone at a nearby bar. He kept on playing with his martini glass and looking at our Susan. Then, speaking broken English, he invited her to dance; she accepted with pleasure. They danced cheek-to-cheek and, when the rest of us left, Pasquale and Susan sat on a bench under the stars, just like Romeo and Juliet.

CHAPTER 7

THE BEACH! THE LEANING TOWER!

The excitement of the previous day zapped all our energy. I decided my vacationers would greatly benefit from an extra hour of sleep. In the morning, I cheerfully greeted everybody:

"Buon Giorno! Where are we going today? I forgot. Please tell me!"

People laughed and said, "We forgot it too! Let's stay in beautiful Montecatini. We love it!"

After a delicious buffet breakfast, we continued on to our next adventure: we boarded our bus and aimed west towards Pisa. There were pink and white oleanders in bloom along the freeway. Yes, the Italian freeways are very well-maintained and adorned with flowers, but they are not *free*, the toll is rather high.

Mariano had been driving for about ten minutes when I shouted: "The Leaning Tower! Look, there on your left!"

Heads turned and everyone chuckled: "Not the tower we expected!"

I fooled them only for seconds. We were passing by a door and window factory, which displayed a huge door that was *leaning* indeed.

Later, as we passed by a billboard with a giant picture of *Pinocchio,* I shouted again: "Look, there is my friend, Pinocchio, and this is not a joke."

Pinocchio was born in the nearby mountain town of Collodi. Yes, he lived there, went to school there, helped his father, Geppetto, and is now buried in Collodi! In fact, the locals have made of that town a *Pinocchioland* for children and adults. I explained in Pisa they sell a multitude of Pinocchio statues. One particular statue represents him with one hand pointing out to his normal nose and another hand holding a quite long nose. When someone at home tells a lie, you can make him/her understand you are aware of it by simply replacing the normal nose with the long one!

Some 2000 years ago, the Romans built aqueducts to carry water from the mountains to the cities. One of those aqueducts with 400 tall arches carried water to Lucca and it can still be seen along the freeway. I warned: "We are getting closer. Prepare your eyes," and then: "There it is! Look on both sides of the road."

This time it was no joke for sure. Everyone saw the ancient aqueduct and marveled. "I can't believe those structures are still standing," remarked Luigi.

"How far is it to the beach?" Mary asked.

"In about twenty minutes, you will be doing *splish and splash* in the water!" I replied.

About ten minutes later, Joan sadly remarked, "It must be quite cold on the beach today. Look at the snow on the mountain!"

I anticipated that remark, but kept quiet. Others looked at the white mountain and were concerned the beach might be too cold. The white on the mountain was not snow, but white marble of the *Apuan Alps*! Since the time of the Romans, people have been ripping open the mountains to extract marble. Seen from a distance, that *white material* appears to be snow. The marble of the *Carrara* quarries is famous for its quality. Over the centuries, many artists have gone there to get material for their artworks. Michelangelo's masterpieces ("La Pieta'", "David", "Moses", etc.) were made with Carrara marble.

Finally, *the beach, the beach*! Italy possesses some of the most beautiful sandy, clean, spacious, and well-organized beaches in the world. The beach in Viareggio is one of them.

"Prepare your feet; the beach is right there!" I said. In their excitement, most people stomped the floor with their feet. Although it was mid-September, we saw many people on the beach and in the water. The sky was completely clear, and the sun warmed the sand. My enthusiastic people ran to the water; there was *splish and splash* everywhere! Others lay on a towel and basked under the warm Tuscan sun. They returned to the bus later, refreshed and relaxed.

From the beach, we drove to Pisa. During the short drive, the *Leaning Tower* was on everybody's mind. To understand what inspired people to build that *wonder of the world*, one must learn the history of Pisa. During the lengthy period of *city-states* of the 11th, 12th, and 13th centuries, Pisa became a mighty maritime independent republic. It maintained a powerful fleet and conducted an intensive trade business with the Orient. Just like the Venetians on the eastern coast of the Italian peninsula, from the western coast Pisa's merchants traveled everywhere and brought back new products, ideas, and artistic styles. As a testament to the wealth of the city, at the peak of its political and economic splendor, Pisa embellished itself with magnificent medieval constructions. Those architectural masterpieces are contained in the *Campo dei Miracoli* (Field of Miracles), where the Leaning Tower is located.

Captain Mariano dropped us off at the tourist bus parking lot. A shuttlebus took us by an imposing medieval wall. From there we walked to an old city gate and entered *Campo dei Miracoli.* Suddenly, *The Leaning Tower, The Duomo, The Baptistery,* and *The Camposanto,* all made of white marble, appeared to us as a real miracle of the Italian engineering and architecture.

The Bell Tower of the Cathedral, known as the Leaning Tower, immediately caught everybody's attention. It looks like a massive wedding cake made of white marble. What mainly attracts people's curiosity is not its artistic value, but the simple fact the tower *leans* to one side and has been for the past 800 years. Today, it represents the symbol and glory of Pisa. When foreign visitors first see the tower, they stand in admiration. The Italian tourists instinctively sing:

"Evviva la Torre di Pisa che pende, che pende e mai casca giu." (Long live the Leaning Tower of Pisa which leans, leans, and never falls down).

It happened that, when the first three floors of the Tower were completed in 1174, the south side sank because the ground was too soft beneath. All work was suspended. One hundred years later the project was resumed and completed as originally planned. Today, it leans seventeen feet out of the perpendicular line. Modern technology is trying to ensure the tower does not fall. If it falls, the symbol of Pisa and its huge tourist business will fall too.

Tourists can go to the top of the Leaning Tower if they climb 296 steps and purchase a rather expensive ticket. A thrilling experience and marvelous view is the reward. If climbing to the top is not possible, some people reward themselves with an unusual photo: stand about 300 feet from the tower, hold up your right hand, and align it with the distant leaning tower. Have someone take a picture of you in that position. You will have a pleasant surprise: the picture will show you are holding the tower from falling down!

Next to the Leaning Tower stands the *cathedral*, built in 1064. It is entirely made of brilliant marble, even the outside walls and sidewalk. The interior is so richly decorated with sculptures and mosaics that it is considered more of a museum than a church; in fact, except during Sunday's religious services, one must pay an entrance fee.

On the left side of the cathedral one finds the *Camposanto* (cemetery), built more than 700 years ago. The wealthy people of Pisa wanted to be buried in the *Holy Land*, but that being impossible, their ships carried tons of *holy soil* from Golgotha and poured it inside the Camposanto. Today, visitors can see tombs, old frescoes, sculptures, sarcophagi, and funerary monuments.

After a brief historic introduction to those architectural *miracles*, we enjoyed some free time. Some people rushed to the Leaning Tower, while others dispersed in all directions, took pictures, bought souvenirs, and ate a *gelato*. I relaxed at an outside café, had a cappuccino, and watched people passing by. At a certain moment, I heard someone calling my name. It was Laura waving from the top of the tower. I yelled: "Don't stand on the leaning side; it might fall down!"

At our Belvedere Hotel, we had another great dinner and then we strolled downtown. While I was sitting at an outdoor café, I saw Susan and Pasquale passing by. I pretended not to see them, but I heard Pasquale say:

"Susanna, you are my Bella Bambinella (Beautiful Baby). Your lips are like inner petals of roses." They walked slowly and then disappeared among the crowd, under the stars.

Nick, sitting next to me, sang a Frank Sinatra's classic: "Strangers in the Night".

Pisa: the Leaning Tower

CHAPTER 8

FLORENCE, THE CRADLE OF RENAISSANCE

The ancient name of *Florence* is *Florentia*, which means *blossoming, blooming, flourishing*. Thus, Florence (in Italian *Firenze*) stands for a *City of Flowers*. However, let us not think of it as a city with flowers in every window, like an Alpine Swiss town. Just like flowers blossom during a certain time of the year, Florence blossomed about 600 years ago, during the time in history called *The Renaissance* and produced the greatest harvest of painters, sculptors, architects, scientists, artisans, goldsmiths, craftsmen, and writers. Their creations filled the museums and churches of Florence and made of it the world's art capital.

Yes, the name Florence brings immediately to mind the arts, and people imagine finding them in every corner of the city. True, a few artistic items can be seen in public places, especially in Piazza Signoria; it is also true many tourists visit the Uffizi Gallery and see the David of Michelangelo. But one should see the more than eighty museums and numerous medieval churches to have a full picture of what the Florentine artistic patrimony is all about. Unfortunately, tourists have a very limited time in Florence, and most of them prefer to spend it shopping, eating in cozy restaurants, or just wandering around. Yet, even that mere presence in the "City of Arts" is sufficient to create in visitors a sincere motivation to learn more about Florence, its arts, and its artists.

Before we go any further, we need to understand the meaning of the term "art". What is art? From Latin, art is a *skill*; therefore, it is a human skill to imitate the nature by creating things that are beautiful and pleasing to look at or to listen to. That creation is mostly expressed through painting, sculpture, architecture, music, and writing. People who exercise that skill are called "artists".

Earth is full of wonderful creations; they are all made by the *Supreme Artist*. The works of art we admire in Florence are all made by humans, and that is what we are going to discover on Day Seven of our tour.

On the way to Florence, the anticipation among my thirty-five "would-be artists" was very high. I heard them say:

"Florence, open your gates! Here we come!"

"Michelangelo, wake up your gorgeous son, David!"

"Dante, I will bring Beatrice back to your arms."

"I am going to buy all of the gold in Florence."

Mario sang: "Mona Lisa, Mona Lisa, are you warm, are you real or just a cold and lovely piece of art?"

Those people sounded like a happy bunch of high school kids. While the bus rolled, I announced a local guide, Serena, was going to walk us through Florence and tell us all about its history and art treasures.

"Does she speak English?" Bruno inquired.

"Of course she does, since you don't understand Italian."

"How old is she? Is she pretty?" Luigi wanted to know.

"She is in her late forties. She is a History and Arts professor. Luigi, would I hire her if she was not pretty?"

"Good. I want a picture with her!"

When we approached the outskirts of Florence, I asked, "Who invented the airplane?" "The Wright Brothers," they answered.

"Wrong. It was Leonardo da Vinci some 500 years ago. He made two light wings, attached them to his arms, climbed to the cliff you see on your left, ran, jumped, and up and away he went!"

Someone interrupted me, shouting, "There is Florence! I can see its red roof dome!"

Tourist buses are required to drop off people at Torre Zecca by the Arno River. From there to the famous Ponte Vecchio, there is a rather long walk. However, because of their eagerness and the pleasant view along the river, people did not notice the distance.

Proceeding along the wall of the right bank of Arno, we walked in front of elegant palaces, luxurious hotels, and a couple of museums. All those buildings had heavy bars on all first-floor windows. We passed by a parking lot with hundreds of motor scooters. In the river, we could see a few rowing-boats gliding silently. Several ducks and catfish followed us along the water; were they welcoming us or looking for food? Some locals were sunbathing and others walking their dogs in a grassy area along the shore. The left side of the river had many colorful palaces with red roofs, green shutters, and blossoming vines. A green hill with pine trees, olive groves, and wisteria provided a picturesque background to those buildings. It was amazing to see the azure sky and the beautiful palaces perfectly reflected in the clear and calm water of Arno.

The banks of Arno, decorated with beautiful antique lamps, are an ideal place for families and friends to stroll in the evening. They are also a favorite setting for lovers to meet at night under a blanket of stars. The famous folk singer Carlo Buti, known as "The Golden Voice of Italy", immortalized the Arno River:

"Quando il sole se ne va, quante coppie innamorate, stretti stretti, cuore a cuore, sul Lungarno come un fiore fioriran…" (After sunset, many couples in a tight embrace, heart to heart, blossom along the Arno like flowers).

When we arrived to *Ponte alle Grazie* we caught sight of the famous covered *Ponte Vecchio* (Old Bridge). The bridge is an odd structure resting on three massive pillars with an agglomeration of superimposed rows of rooms built on top of it. Most rooms are of golden red color with pale green shutters by the windows. Amazingly, several small additional rooms could be seen on the back of the shops, overhanging the river, and supported only by wooden brackets. The unique architecture of Ponte Vecchio makes of it one of the most famous bridges in the world.

At the entrance of the bridge, we found a large crowd of tourists walking, taking pictures, window-shopping, and admiring the river. Searching the crowd with impatient eyes, I found our guide and introduced her to the group. "Ladies and Gentlemen, this is *Signorina Serena*, the best guide in Florence!"

"Remo, you are too generous," she replied. She greeted everybody warmly, took us to the center of Ponte Vecchio, and, for the next two and half hours, talked about her illustrious city. It is impossible to give an account of everything she said. I'll report only the essential.

"Ladies and Gentlemen," Serena said, "we are standing on the famous bridge called *Ponte Vecchio*. It is the oldest bridge in Florence. Built in 1345, it stands as symbol of this city. An open-air pedestrian-way runs in the center. On both sides, you can see quaint shops. Originally, butchers and fishmongers used them. Since they littered the bridge and the river with offal and other animal refuse, they were replaced with jewelers, goldsmiths, art dealers, and stores for leather goods. Look at the open arches in the middle of the bridge. From there, you can enjoy a wonderful panoramic view of the river and the beautiful palaces. Tourists come here mainly attracted by the uniqueness of this bridge."

"Across the northern top of the bridge, you can see part of the half mile long enclosed *Vasari Corridor*. It was built to link the Palazzo Vecchio to the *Pitti Palace*. About seven hundred paintings decorate the interior of the Corridor; most of them represent prominent people of the Medici family who ruled Florence. Now, look at the bronze statue in front of us; it represents Benvenuto Cellini, an ingenious goldsmith and sculptor."

"Serena, what are all those padlocks affixed around the railing of Cellini's statue?" Angela asked.

"Yes, many young people come here to pledge their love. By placing a lock around this railing and throwing the key in the river, the lovers remain eternally locked together."

"How nice! I wish I could do that!" Angela sighed.

"Look at the Arno River; it winds through the city like a golden ribbon and it reflects the buildings along its banks. However, now and then, Arno misbehaves and terrorizes this city. The flood of November 1966 was particularly destructive; the water rose twenty-two feet in the center of the city, killed 101 people, submerged a million books in the National Library, and ruined a thousand paintings and many other historic and artistic treasures."

Florence: Ponte Vecchio

"Before walking through the city," Serena said, "let me give you a brief history of Florence. About 2600 years ago, this area was an Etruscans settlement. Later, the Romans took over and named it *Florentia*, which means *flourishing*. In fact, soon it flourished into a prominent city. After the fall of the Roman Empire, it barely survived under the barbarian rule, but, from the 11th century onwards, Florentia gained its autonomy and organized itself under the government of powerful families. Overcoming the rivalry of the neighboring city-states of Pisa, Siena, Arezzo, Pistoia, and Volterra, Florence expanded its territory to what is the present Tuscany region. Today, the city has a population of about half million."

"By the beginning of the 14th century, Florence became one of the most important economic and cultural centers of Italy. After an extended period of internal fighting with the advent of *Cosimo the Elder* in 1434, the glorious ruling power of the Medici family began. Their rule lasted for more than three hundred years. During that time, the Medici encouraged and patronized artists, men of letters, and scientists. Thus began the period of civilization known as *Renaissance*, which means 'rebirth' or 'return' to the artistic and literary values of the Greek and Roman ancient culture. After a long period of splendor and independence, in 1860 Tuscany and its capital Florence volunteered to join the newly formed Italian Kingdom."

We followed our gentle guide along the pedestrian street *Por Santa Maria* and entered the historic center; it was literally packed with tourists. We walked close to Serena and asked questions. While holding an elderly lady by the arm, she pointed out some remarkable palaces.

We stopped by a busy market where we saw a group of people laughing and taking pictures of something. We went closer and saw the bronze statue of a huge wild boar, called *Porcellino*. Tourists rub his snout and place a coin into his gaping jaws. They say it will assure your return to Florence.

"Here, Porcellino, bring me back to Florence!" Sandra sighed, dropping a coin in his jaw.

Next to the Porcellino stands an outdoor market that attracts many bargain hunters. There, one can find crafts, clothing, laces, embroidery, straw hats, leather goods, t-shirts, souvenirs, and other tourist related items.

After a short walk through Via Calimaruzza, we entered a large, public square with imposing and colorful palaces. Many restaurants with outside tables served coffee, cold drinks, and delicious snacks. A couple of policemen wearing dark pants, blue uniforms, and white helmets kept a watchful eye on the crowd. A few horse-drawn, brownish carriages waited for passengers. Some coachmen napped while their horses contentedly kept on eating hay in a bag hanging from their neck. Many tourists took pictures or were listening to their guide. We, too, stood by our guide, as she described the Piazza and its content.

"This is *Piazza della Signoria*, the political heart of medieval Florence," said Serena. For many centuries, it was used as a setting for public speeches, ceremonies, meetings, and executions. As you can see, there are a lot of classy shops and cafés. The buildings and the numerous sculptures you see here make of this square an *open-air museum*, evoking Florence's centuries of greatness and power. The colossal, brownish palace in front of us is *Palazzo Vecchio*, designed by Arnolfo di Cambio in 1299. It looks more like a fortress than a palace and it has not changed ever since. For about seven hundred years, it served as official seat of government. Look at the Latin inscription above the main entrance door; it reads, 'Rex Regum et Dominus Dominantium' (King of Kings and Lord of Lords). That is the proud title the rulers of this city gave themselves. The tall tower rising above it is 800 years old. You can climb to the top and admire unforgettable views, if you are not scared of going 308 feet high."

"Now, look at that bronze equestrian monument on the far left of the Square; it is a monument to *Cosimo the First* by Giambologna. He was the founder of the Medici power in Florence."

We noticed Cosimo was so absorbed in the thought of his good old days, he did not feel the presence of a pigeon resting on his head and another one on his hand!

Our guide continued lecturing about the several statues displayed in Piazza Signoria. She pointed out the statue of *Neptune,* a masterpiece of Ammannati. His countrymen did not like it and nicknamed it *Biancone* (Big Whitey). They even made fun of the sculptor: "Ammannato, Ammannato, che bel marmo hai rovinato!" (What a nice piece of marble you have ruined).

"Now, look at the marble statue of *David* by Michelangelo," said Serena, "it symbolizes Florence's strength and liberty from tyranny. However, what you see here is a copy; the real David was moved to the Galleria dell' Accademia in 1873." (We will talk about him in the next chapter).

"Serena," interrupted Susan, "David was a Jew. Why isn't he circumcised? Look at him!"

Serena blushed and replied: "I don't have an answer. Since his father, Michelangelo, was Italian, perhaps he didn't want him circumcised."

Another colossal statue represented *Hercules and Cacus* by Bandinelli. Right behind it, an attentive tourist can discover a bas-relief profile of a head sculpted in the stone of the wall. They say Michelangelo was such a talented artist, he sculpted that image with his back on the wall.

Serena called our attention to the brownish building with three high and wide arches on the right side of the Square. "That is the *Loggia dei Lanzi*. It was built in 1376 to hold public ceremonies under cover. Later it was enriched with many sculptures. Look at the two lions guarding the entrance. Under the left arch, you see the statue of Perseus killing Medusa; it is a masterpiece of Cellini. Also notice Judith and Holofernes, Hercules, and the Centaur, Menelaus sustaining the body of Patroclus and the kidnapping of the Sabine Women. Look also at the other remarkable statues on the back of the Loggia. Today, this Loggia is a real open-air museum." Serena told us the history attached to each statue.

Several tourists were inside the Loggia, looking at the statues, taking pictures or sitting on the steps. A peevish attendant supervised the entire area. We noticed he was acting as if he was *somebody:* any time he had the opportunity to reprimand a tourist, he ran to admonish "No eating, no drinking in the Loggia!"

On the right side of Palazzo Vecchio, Serena showed us a long courtyard with two magnificent palaces. On the exterior walls, there were numerous niches with the statue of many masters of the Renaissance. Nearby a few mimes, impersonating some leading artists, had hard time to attract people's attention. The mine impersonating Cupid had a better luck: many women wanted a picture of themselves being transfixed by Cupid's arrow. Another mime, posing as a homeless, was shaking a noise-maker gadget to show he was alive and not a statue. A few onlookers admired the caricatures drawn by street artists.

Pointing out said palace, our guide Serena explained, "That is the *Uffizi Gallery,* the oldest museum in the world. It contains more than 4800 works of the highest achievements of western art. A large number of famous artists of the Renaissance have their masterpieces displayed there. To name a few: Cimabue, Giotto, Duccio, Martini, Lippi, Botticelli, Leonardo, Cellini, Bellini, Correggio, Tiziano, Caravaggio, Tintoretto, Raffaello, Michelangelo."

"Can we visit the museum now?" Antoinette asked.

"Not now. You must stand in line to get the ticket and then you need to spend an entire day inside there."

Back to Piazza della Signoria, Serena stopped by a reddish circular plaque on the ground, and said, "You must know that politically it was not all glorious in Florence. It was dangerous to oppose the Medici or any other ruling party. The famous poet, Dante Alighieri, was exiled because of his political views. Now, look at the round porphyry plaque right where Betty is standing; that is the exact spot where on May 23, 1498 the monk *Girolamo Savonarola* was burned at the stake for opposing the Medici. His ashes were then thrown in the Arno River."

"Good Heavens!" Betty screamed and jumped back, as if she was on fire.

While we stood on Piazza Signoria, a parade came our way; they were celebrating 150-year anniversary of the city's *polizia* (police). There was a band playing patriotic music and a lengthy line of policemen, all in traditional uniform, riding on horseback while others were marching.

Signorina Serena walked us through the prestigious *Via dei Calzaiuoli,* open only to pedestrians. It is the most central and most elegant street of Florence; a kind of outdoor shopping mall. Serena pointed out a few magnificent and historic palaces housing high fashion shops and restaurants on the ground level. Luxurious residences are on the upper floors. Via dei Calzaiuoli is also an elegant street bustling with tourists taking pictures and glancing at every store. Several local, classy ladies were seen carrying shopping bags loaded with newly acquired clothes.

Following their guide, a couple of hasty tourist groups passed in front of us. A horse-drawn carriage with a romantic couple had hard time to make his way among the crowd; quite often he had to sound a rubber hooter with his foot. Standing by some pastry shops, a few tourists praised the quality of food. Mary and Sandra were tempted to stop for a *gelato*, but they were afraid of losing sight of their group.

"Serena, why are those graffiti on the street?" Joan enquired.

"Oh no, dear lady, those are not graffiti. Those are marvelous works made by street artists, called *Madonnari*. Using chalk pastels, they recreate sacred images and icons on the pavement of the street."

Many tourists stop there, watch, take pictures, and drop coins in a basket.

At the end of Via dei Calzaiuoli, we suddenly came in front of a gigantic and spectacular building that took everybody's breath away.

"Oh, my God! What is that?"

"How beautiful!"

"It makes me cry!"

"It gives me goosebumps!"

"It is gorgeous! Serena, what is that?"

Serena called for everybody's attention, and explained, "Oh, yes. It is gorgeous indeed! This extraordinary building is the *Church of Santa Maria del Fiore*, known as *Duomo* or cathedral. It is the greatest architectural marvel of the Florentine Renaissance and the fourth largest Christian church. It measures 502 feet long and 381 feet high. I can hold 30,000 people inside. Many great artists worked on it, but it owes its existence mostly to *Arnolfo di Cambio*. Construction began in 1296 and was finished 200 years later. Look at its magnificent façade; it is made entirely of green, white and pink marble, same colors as the Italian flag."

"The *Cupola* is an absolute miracle of Renaissance engineering. Imagine: it was built without the use of scaffolds. It is a creation of the architect *Filippo Brunelleschi*. If you can climb its 463 steps, you will enjoy a breathtaking view of the city and surrounding area." We could see people on top of the Cupola.

"Due to the long line, we are not going inside the Duomo, but I recommend you visit it during your free time. Inside, you will find many works of art, tombstones, stained-glass- windows, and an interesting painting of "The Last Judgment". Don't miss seeing the astronomical

Clock of Paolo Uccello, above the main entrance door; it has been counting the hours since 1443."

The Piazza in front of the Duomo bustled with tourists taking pictures, reading a guidebook, or listening to a tour guide. Many sat on the steps of the church or stood in line to get inside. A few young gypsy girls, with colorful long dresses, came around us, jingling a paper cup, and asking for money. Eventually, they would attempt to steal wallets and cameras from distracted tourists. I kept on chasing them away: "Vai, via!" (Go away).

Right across from the cathedral we admired the 1300-year-old *Baptistery*. Serena stopped in front of its gleaming eastern door and began lecturing with a witty remark.

"Ladies and Gentlemen, you are almost in Heaven! Look at this door; it is called 'The Gate of Paradise'. Sculptured by *Lorenzo Ghiberti* in 1425, it is a true masterpiece of the Renaissance goldsmith's craft and is one of the most famous works of art in the world. It contains ten wonderful *golden panels* representing scenes from the Old Testament. Beginning with the panel on the top left, you can see 'The Creation of Adam and Eve', 'Noah', 'Jacob', 'Moses', 'David', 'Cain and Abel', 'Abraham', 'Joseph', 'Joshua', and 'Solomon'. Ghiberti worked on this exquisite door for twenty-seven years. However, this is a copy; the original gate is kept in the Museum of the Duomo."

Next to the cathedral, we saw the graceful *Campanile* (Bell Tower), beautifully clad in white marble from Carrara, green marble from Prato and red marble from Siena. The campanile was designed in 1334 by *Giotto*, a famous painter and architect. There are 450 steps to get to the top at a height of 277 feet.

We walked along the right side of the Duomo and passed by two colossal statues.

"Holy moly! Who are these guys?" Peter wondered.

"This one is Arnolfo di Cambio," said Serena. "He started the construction of the Duomo. The other one is Brunelleschi who built the Cupola."

Florence: Duomo

Passing by the *Sasso di Dante* (Dante's Stone), Serena told us: "Dante sat here for hours, while watching the construction of the Duomo and writing love poems for Beatrice. A folktale tells an interesting anecdote. One day, while Dante was sitting on this stone, an unknown Florentine accosted him and asked: 'What do you like for breakfast?'

'Hard boiled eggs,' he replied.

A year later, the same man asked again: 'With what?'

'With salt,' Dante quickly responded."

"Serena, some churches are called 'cathedrals', some 'basilicas', and some 'duomos'. What is the difference?" Mario inquired.

"Cathedral comes from the Latin *Cathedra,* and means 'seat'. Thus, a cathedral is a church with a bishop's seat; there is a bishop in residence. *Duomo* derives from the Latin term *Domus* and means 'house', thus house of God. It is just a title granted to some prominent churches. *Basilica* comes from Greek term *Basileus* (king) and it designates a large, sumptuous church (like a king's palace) that has been given that title because of its architectural or religious importance. Thus, Duomo and Basilica are just titles; they may have also a bishop's seat, but not necessarily."

A few people showed signs of fatigue, but our guide kindly encouraged them, reassuring the tour would soon end. We had only a few more interesting sights to visit. In the narrow, medieval *Via dello Studio* we felt dwarfed among high stone palaces. At a certain point, Peter stopped in front of a small niche and could not figure out what it was.

"That is a 'Tabernacle'," explained Serena. "We have many of them in Florence, especially at the corner of public streets or on the façade of private houses, shops, and buildings. They contain a painted image of the Virgin Mary or St. John the Baptist, the city's patrons. The tabernacles are a constant reminder to the passers-by to keep the devotion to those saints."

A few steps further, and we entered a small, austere church made of dark stones. A low light and a soft music gave the interior a mystical feeling, like a little oasis of peace from the bustle of the city.

Speaking in a low voice, Serena explained, "This is the *Church of Dante*. Here, he experienced love at first sight for Beatrice, but his love was never returned; she married someone else and died at the age of twenty-four. She was buried under this altar on June 8, 1290. After her death, Dante was devastated; he could not find peace until he started his literary work, the *Divine Comedy*, in which he described her as 'Woman-Angel' with an ideal beauty and grace. He called her 'Lode di Dio vera' (True Glory of God) and 'Beata, Bella' (Blessed, Pretty) with eyes that shine brighter than the stars. Now, this tiny church has become a symbolic shrine for lovers with broken hearts. In fact, next to her tomb, you can see a basket full of messages for Beatrice, asking help to regain the lost love."

Immediately, Angela sat on a pew, got a pen and a scrap of paper, and wrote: "Please, Beatrice, help me get my Giorgio back. I can't stand losing him." She kissed that paper and placed it on the very top of the basket. I think it would be more appropriate if those love notes were addressed to Dante, since he, not Beatrice, had a broken heart.

Not far from Beatrice's chapel, on Via Santa Margherita, we saw a three-story building made of dark stones. A man, dressed in medieval clothes, recited verses from the "Divine Comedy."

"You are now looking at the paternal 'House of Dante Alighieri'," Serena told us. "He was born here in 1265. He is the most beloved Italian poet, founder of the Italian language, and one of the world's greatest writers. Unfortunately, the Florentines banished him because of his political views. He died in Ravenna in 1321. Dante is also the father of the Italian language. After the fall of the Roman Empire, Latin was spoken in Italy for many more centuries, but, with the advent of the barbarian hordes, it became a low Latin. Through the ages, it was spoken differently in many parts of the Italian peninsula. Finally, the Italian scholars decided to adopt Dante's language as national language."

"Florence banished, but did not forget its greatest son. In fact, it attempted in vain to bring his body back. Today, more than thirty plaques with excerpts of his literary masterpiece can be seen framed in front of many palaces."

Our guide walked us through the medieval Via del Corso, Via Proconsolo, and Via Dell'Anguillara, where we found many restaurants, cafés, and *trattorie* crowded with people enjoying pasta, pizza, and wine; it made our mouths water. We passed by the Bargello Museum and by the Gondi Palace, where Leonardo da Vinci resided for a while and painted the *Mona Lisa*. Imagine: today that painting is worth at least one billion dollars!

Finally, *Santa Croce Square* appeared like another prodigy of the medieval Florentine architecture. On three sides the Square has picturesque palaces with walls plastered in dark khaki color. Several stores sell leather goods and gold items. The restaurants and outdoor cafés in that Square are constantly crowded with tourists. A stop at Santa Croce Square offers the visitors the last chance to shop before returning to their bus; in fact, many bargain hunters can be seen rushing from one store to the other and fill their bags like Christmas shoppers.

With a charming smile, our gentle guide took us in front of a huge and old church, located on the eastern side of the Square. She told us: "This is Santa Croce Church. I consider it the most important church in the city. We Florentines proudly call it 'The temple of the Italian glories', because it contains the tomb of some of the most illustrious Italians who have made Florence and Italy famous throughout the world. We have no time to go inside, but I recommend you visit it on your own and stop in front of each tomb. Michelangelo's resting place is the first one on the right, as you enter. He died in Rome in 1564, at the age of eighty-nine. The Florentines, determined to have him back, stole his body and smuggled it under bales of hay. Next, you can see the monument of Dante; he died in 1321 and is buried in Ravenna. The tomb of Niccolo' Macchiavelli is there too. The famous composer Gioacchino Rossini is buried there. The great astronomer, Galileo Galilei, the poets Ugo Foscolo and Vittorio Alfieri, Lorenzo Ghiberti, Enrico Fermi, Guglielmo Marconi, and many other famous artists and thinkers have their tombs along the walls of this memorable church."

"My dear Ladies and Gentlemen, our walking tour is over. I wish you could stay longer and see the precious content of our numerous museums. I wish I could talk to you about our artistic treasures for two and half days instead of two and half hours. I greatly appreciate the interest you showed during this brief time. I see you have gained a sincere desire to learn more about arts. Grazie. And now, my dears, I declare each of you 'Honorary Citizens' of my beloved Florence. Grazie and God bless you."

"Grazie, Professor Serena. In such a short time, you have inspired and enlightened our minds and hearts," I replied.

Immediately, everybody gave her a sincere applause and a warm embrace. Yes, Luigi and a few other men had a picture taken with Serena. It was about 1:00 p.m.

I called everybody's attention: "Hear me, hear me. Now you have free time. Regroup in front of this church at four o'clock."

"Where is a good place to eat?" asked Karen.

"Karen, I don't recommend any particular restaurant because there are so many and they are all good. You decide which one appeals to your appetite. Notice that in Italy there is *no sales tax*. If waiters add it to your bill and give you tough time, call me and I will rescue you.

78

Know, however, that it is customary to charge for *pane e coperto* (cover charge and bread), even if you don't eat bread."

"Remo, when can I see my gorgeous David?" Betty wanted to know.

"If you give up your lunch, you will have time to see him now. If you wait until tomorrow you will have more time."

At 4:00 p.m., sharp, my tired, but cheerful, thirty-five *Honorary Florentine Citizens* reappeared from everywhere; most of them carried a heavy shopping bag. Through a short-cut on Via San Giuseppe and then Via dei Malcontenti, we went back to Torre Zecca. There, I heard Sandra timidly whining:

"Where is the bus? Why isn't Mariano here?"

"Patience, Sandra. Tourist buses are not allowed to stop and wait. They have only a few minutes to drop off and pick up people. We must wait for the bus and not vice versa." Then, I told the group: "When you board the bus, do it quickly. Do not stop by the door trying to make your point about something: there is no *point* in making your *point* at that *point*!"

"And that is a good *point*!" added Tony.

After such a tiring, but educational day, at our Hotel Belvedere dinner and wine were more than welcomed. We had a delicious antipasto, spaghetti with meat sauce, and roast loin of veal with potatoes and spinach. For dessert, we had a delicious *tiramisu*. Wine was included.

When our waiter, Antonio, saw Luisa was not eating her tiramisu, he asked, "Don't you like it?"

She said she did like it, but she was going to eat a *gelato* at an outside café.

He replied, "Aspetta," (wait) and then brought her a nice, big dish of gelato. She gave him a kiss and, of course, Antonio reciprocated immediately.

Talking about romance, after dinner most of us walked downtown Montecatini and sat in an outside bar. We saw Susan and Pasquale passing by; they held hands, and I believe they spent another romantic evening under the Tuscan moon.

"Ah! Amore, Amore! (Love, Love!) She is a lucky woman!" Linda sighed.

Our Florence Guide Serena

CHAPTER 9

FLORENCE AND TUSCAN WINERY

Even though on Day Eight of our tour my gentle people had a very exciting experience in Florence, their dreams were not totally fulfilled. Some wanted to see David, while others had shopping in mind. In the morning, I heard them say:

"Today, I am going on a shopping spree!"

"I want to see my sweetheart, David!"

"I will sit in a cozy restaurant, eat pizza, and drink a gallon of Chianti!"

It was Sunday, and many went to the church of St. Francis in Montecatini. At 9:30, we bid farewell to our kind hosts at Hotel Belvedere. The sun was radiant and the traffic very light, therefore, we made it downtown rather quickly. Our bus dropped us off at Torre Zecca. We took a shortcut and reached Santa Croce Square, where we were the day before.

Standing on a concrete bench, I shouted, "Come closer! Hear me! Now you have three hours of free time. Be back here at one o'clock. Ciao."

Some people had a clear idea of what they were going to do; others needed help.

"Remo, seven of us are going to see gorgeous David. Where is he?" Linda asked.

"Well, on Sunday he gets up late, but, by the time you get there, he should be ready to receive visitors. Go to the left side of the Duomo and walk along Via Ricasoli until you see the museum called *Galleria dell'Accademia*. Handsome David has been living there since 1873. By the way, ask his father Michelangelo why he is not circumcised!"

Some information about that most-admired statue in the world is useful at this point. Gorgeous David was born in Florence in 1504. Michelangelo was only twenty-nine when he gave life to that sixteen-foot son. Although he is now more than 500 years old, he looks as good as the day he was born. Florentines say the secret to his youth is he eats only spaghetti cooked with olive oil and drinks only Chianti wine!

David's beautiful and robust body fascinates visitors. Some people claim he brings tears to their eyes when they first see him. In fact, if you stare at him for a while, you have the impression, at any moment, he is going to step down from the podium and greet his admirers.

When the statue of David was completed, it was placed in front of Palazzo della Signoria as a symbol of the city's pride and liberty. There, he remained ravaged by wind and rain for almost 400 years. He also had to tolerate people staring at his most private parts. Finally, after centuries of abuse, in 1873 he was given a good cleansing and brought into a more comfortable residence in the Galleria dell'Accademia. The statue we see today on the same podium in Piazza Signoria is only a copy, perhaps David's cousin.

Most ladies in the group were not interested in gorgeous David; they had been anxiously waiting for some free time to do their shopping. I took them to *Peruzzi*, right in front of Santa Croce Square. Peruzzi is a large store with three floors. One can find everything in there: leather goods, handbags, shoes, gold, jewelry, clothes, souvenirs, copies of major art works, and things with the Florence label. They also have clean and free restrooms.

A few women asked directions to *San Lorenzo Market*.

I told them: "Go to the front of the Duomo, take Via Martelli, turn left at Palazzo Medici and there you will find it."

St. Lawrence Market is a picturesque half mile long shopping place; it has a large display of stalls where one can find clothes, bags, shoes, belts, hats, gloves, luggage, etc. The price of those items is very reasonable, but the quality might not be genuine.

"Remo, I have a good friend in Salerno; could I go there during this free time?" enquired Tom.

"Do you mean Salerno, the city near Naples?"

"Yes, that's it! That is what he said."

"Dear Tom, if you drive a car, you would barely get there late tonight! When we get to Capri, you can go there."

"Oh, no. I cannot miss Capri!"

Sometimes people don't understand the actual distances between cities. Tom thought Salerno was near Florence! During their free time, two of my men climbed the cathedral's Dome; two others went to the top of Giotto's Campanile. No one bothered to go to the Uffizi Museums; there wasn't enough time, unless they had already purchased their tickets. Paula and Anne did not feel like walking; they asked how to get to Piazza Signoria.

"We will sit somewhere in there," they said.

"I will walk with you there," I comforted them. Later, when I saw them still sitting in the same outdoor café, they called me over and treated me to a traditional Florentine lunch.

Precisely at 1:30 p.m., everyone was at the meeting place. Linda could not refrain from talking about her gorgeous David.

"Well, what he got that my husband doesn't," Joan objected.

"Youth and beauty!" replied Linda.

Everyone laughed.

Before leaving that glorious city, we drove by *Piazzale Michelangelo*, which is on a hill by the Arno River. The Piazzale offers a stunning view of the city.

Some people sighed: "Arrivederci, Bella Firenze!"

On the southern outskirts of Florence, we drove by an enormous monastery located on top of a grassy hill; it is *La Certosa* built in 1341. That reminded me to tell this funny story.

"In olden times, the monks in that monastery had to make the vow of silence. They could only talk to confess their sins and to yell 'Fuoco!' (Fire!), if there was a fire. However, every ten years they were permitted to speak three words. Once, after ten years of silence, Brother Rocco was asked to say his three words in front of the community.

'Bed too hard,' complained Brother Rocco. The father superior took note and ten years later asked:

'Brother Rocco, what do you have to say?'

'Food always stinks.'

Ten years later: 'Brother Rocco, speak your three words.'

'Now I quit.'

'I bet you quit. You have been complaining for the past thirty years!' commented the father superior."

At Pierluigi's Tuscan Cantina

Next, I made a phone call:

"Ciao. Pierluigi, come stai? Saremo da te fra poco". (Hello, Pierluigi, how are you? We will be there in a little while). *Pierluigi* is the owner of a *Winery* located in the town of Torciano, between Florence and Siena. We were going there for an afternoon of wine and fun.

Mariano drove us through the scenic Tuscan countryside strewn with rolling green hills covered with beautiful vineyards, gnarled olive trees, large fields of sunflowers and rows of cypress trees around stone farm houses. Quaint medieval villages could be seen at every turn of the road.

"Oh, how I wish to have a villa in these hills and live just like Romeo and Juliette!" Mary sighed.

We arrived near the town of Torciano situated in the heart of Tuscany. "There, can you see that big hill covered with vineyards?" I asked. "Pierluigi owns all that. I have a big surprise for you."

When we entered *Tenuta Torciano* (Torciano Estate), a shaggy little dog welcomed us at the gate. Then, Mira, Pierluigi's sister, wearing a bright red dress and brown sandals, walked toward us. Her black hair was pulled back with a white and green ribbon. She hugged me and greeted everybody very warmly.

Pierluigi is proud to tell his visitors the history of his vineyard. He says his great great great grandfather started the family wine business. He had eighteen children and they all worked in the vineyard. Pierluigi also began working in the vineyard as young man. When recently the American tourists invaded Tuscany, looking for wineries, he had the brilliant idea of transforming his old farmhouse into an old-fashioned "Wine Cellar" with tables inside, outside and in the basement.

In his manicured courtyard Pierluigi has fig, olive, and pomegranate trees. A delightful blend of spices, rosemary, lavender, sage, and bay leaves combined with the scent of roses fill the garden with a heavenly aroma. In a corner behind a fence one can see chickens and ducks. Three friendly cats and a peacock walk freely in the backyard. Empty wine barrels lay along the fence.

We sat outside under a large gazebo. A young man served antipasto: two slices of bread and olive oil, cheese, salami, prosciutto, and olives. Suddenly, just like "Jack in the Box", Pierluigi appeared out of nowhere. He hugged two ladies and greeted us: "Hello, Everybody! Welcome to Tenuta Torciano! I am Pierluigi. You are going to taste the best wine you ever had." He complemented a few ladies on their hair and dress and called them *Queens and Princesses*. Oh, yes, he liked to flirt! He was hilarious, colorful, outgoing and he knew his stuff. Pierluigi looked at one of prettiest ladies and said: "Hello, beautiful. What is your name?"

"I am Rose."

"That is a nice name. Where do you come from, Rose?"

"From Williamsport, PA, sir."

He kissed her on the cheek. "Okay, Rose, please take this bottle of *Sangiovese* wine and pour some in each glass."

She felt honored and served wine singing and toddling.

Pierluigi shouted, "Ladies and Gentlemen, the wine you are going to taste today is produced in my vineyard. On the table, you have a paper listing the eleven various kinds of wine. Next to each kind you have a grading scale from one to ten. As you taste each wine, write down the grade you give it. This first one is called *Sangiovese*. Now, let us have a toast. Salute and Welcome!"

Lecturing on the art of tasting wines, Pierluigi taught us how to hold, swirl, sniff and taste wine. Then he hugged Luisa and asked her to serve the *Classico* wine. Then he complimented Mary's dress and asked her to serve the *Vernaccia* wine. We tasted also *Montepulciano, Chianti,* and more. The eleventh kind of wine was called *Vino Santo* (Holy Wine): that was more than holy, it was divine! In the meanwhile, Mira kept on serving more cheese and salami. A couple of cats tried to steal cheese from our tables. Finally, Pierluigi made us taste some olive oil with truffles and gave us a liqueur called *aphrodisiac*. "This is what you need, not Viagra!" he laughed.

All that fun, food, and wine did not cost us a penny. However, after that joyful party, Pierluigi explained: "I have a distributor in Chicago.

He will deliver wine to your door. If you are interested, fill out this order paper." Of course, he sold a lot of wine!

With his wine, Pierluigi gave us kindness, warmth, and smile. We had a real *barrel of laughs*, much bigger than Pierluigi's wine barrels. People said visiting that winery was yet another highlight of the tour.

Since Pierluigi was too busy selling wine, one by one, all the ladies gave him a warm hug and left; some were rather tipsy. Everybody boarded the bus laughing and praising the winery, but fifteen minutes later they were soundly asleep.

Having fun at the Winery

About an hour later, we entered the *Umbria* region, which means "shady" because of its green hills and mountains. That region is also known as *The Heart of Italy* and *The Etruscan Land*, because the Etruscans lived there some 3000 years ago. In Umbria, one can find many picturesque medieval towns and religious shrines. Unfortunately, most tourists bypass Umbria; they drive straight from Florence to Rome. Yet, one cannot have a complete picture of Italy by visiting only cities crowded with foreign tourists; one must see also places where the *Italians* are. That is why for the next few days we went to the Region of Umbria, Marche, and Abruzzo.

"What do you call a man from Umbria?" I asked.

"Umbriaco!" said John.

"No! Umbriaco in Italian means 'drunk'. You call him 'Umbro'."

"Well, today we are all umbriaco!"

When we drove by *Lago Trasimeno* (Trasimeno Lake), I explained that in 217 BC the famous Carthaginian general *Hannibal* crossed the Alps, descended into Italy with 90,000 foot soldiers, 12,000 cavalry men, and 37 elephants. He ambushed the Romans on the same spot where we were driving and, in less than four hours, annihilated their armies. More than 16,000 men perished in that battle.

John had an interesting question. "I often see police cars. They have different names: *Carabinieri, Polizia, Guardia di Finanza*. What is the difference?"

I explained that *Carabinieri* represented the national police charged with maintaining public security. They wear a uniform in dark blue with silver braid around the collar, edges trimmed in scarlets, and epaulettes in silver. *Polizia* is mostly city police, securing also public order on highway, railways, and airports. *Guardia di Finanza* is the police that controls financial matters and patrols the national borders.

When we came out of a tunnel, the city of *Perugia* appeared on our left, up on the hill. It was a beautiful view. Perugia is known for its candy factories. The chocolate called *Baci Perugini* (Perugia Kisses) are particularly popular in Italy. They are filled with hazelnuts and wrapped in multilingual love notes. They say when you give someone *Baci* you get a *kiss* in return. No wonder those Baci are very popular in Italy! Perugia is to Italy what Hershey is to America.

Soon, the city of *Assisi* could be seen in the distance, perched on the flank of mount Subasio. Since only small cars fit through the narrow, medieval streets of downtown Assisi, new and large hotels are in *Santa*

Maria degli Angeli, a town in the plain, down below Assisi. Our hotel was *Villa Verde* (Green Villa). The owner, Francesco, and his lovely wife, Anna, received us with a "Welcome Drink". The rooms were very clean and had a crucifix above each bed. The walls of the bathrooms were made of glistening white and green marble. Some rooms had three beds to accommodate entire families of pilgrims.

Not only is Villa Verde a neat place, but food there is the best. Dinner began with a *bruschetta* (toasted bread with olive oil); then came a dish of delicious *minestrone* (vegetable soup) and a dish of *rigatoni*. Another dish of pasta with white and spicy *truffle sauce* made everyone drink a lot of wine. When we thought our stomachs were full, the main course was served: steak with roasted potatoes, asparagus, salad, and fruit. To finish that happy meal, waiter Alessandro came around with a cup of ice cream and an after-dinner drink. Many people decided not to eat lunch the next day, so they could, again, enjoy that "square meal". Wine was not included, but it was only five euros per bottle.

We were not alone in that large dining room. Two other groups from Calabria, a region south Italy, were guests of Villa Verde. After dinner, we all moved to the recreation room. An old man played an accordion and made people dance tango, waltz, polka, cha-cha, line dancing, etc. The Calabresi invited us to join them and, except for a few people who said they ate too much, most of us joined them and had fun.

CHAPTER 10

ASSISI: CRADLE OF RELIGIOUS RENAISSANCE

Most High Omnipotent Good Lord, be praised by all your creatures, especially Brother Sun and Sister Earth.

This song resounded in Assisi about 800 years ago. The minstrel singing it was *San Francesco* (Saint Francis). We know that, after the fall of the Roman Empire and under the Barbarians, Man made very little use of his gift of intelligence. Not only his mind, but his religious spirit, fell into ruin. There was the need of someone sent by Heaven to bring Man back to his spiritual life. That someone was Francesco of Assisi. We can say St. Francis was to the *Religious Renaissance* what Michelangelo was to the *Cultural Renaissance*. For 800 years, Assisi has been a sacred place for pilgrims, brown-robbed friars and saintly sightseers.

Assisi is a picturesque medieval town of about 25,000 people. From afar, it looks like a storybook town floating above a hilltop. Mighty ancient walls can still be seen around it. The town has remained intact over the many centuries and time in there seems to have come to a standstill. Walking through its narrow medieval, steep, and narrow streets one feels like stepping back in time at least 1000 years. It seems the words of St. Francis "Pax et Bonum" (Peace and Prosperity) are still tangible everywhere. Today, after 800 years, that lovely place of calm and tranquility still draws pilgrims from all over the world. They go to Assisi to recover their peace of mind by walking on the footsteps of the Saint.

Yes, Assisi is known throughout the world because San Francesco was born there in 1182. He was the son of Pietro Bernardone, a rich clothing merchant, and Mona Pica, a noble French lady. His name was Giovanni, but his father nicknamed him "Francesco" ("Little French-man"). As a young man, Francesco led a carefree life, but God had other plans for him. One day, while praying in the church of St. Damiano, a voice came out of a huge crucifix, and told him:

"Francis, go and repair my church which is falling into ruins."

After some hesitation, Francis understood his mission, adopted a new life modeled on that of Christ and preached the Gospel every-where. He embraced poverty, prayed constantly, worked miracles, healed the sick, and even raised the dead.

When he began preaching, Francesco was mocked and persecuted; even his own father, Pietro Bernardone, gave him a tough time. Pietro attempted to change his mind first with threats, and then with beating and locking him in a dark closet. But soon, Francesco had a large audi-ence and many men followed his life of prayer, penance, and poverty. He preached everywhere and to everybody. He believed nature is the mirror of God; he called all creatures his "brothers" and "sisters". He performed numerous miracles and even tamed a ferocious wolf sowing terror among the people and made of him a city pet. He preached to the birds that listened to him silently and at the end of the sermon stretched out their necks, flapped their wings, and touched his tunic with their beaks. If we lived in Assisi at that time, we could have seen the hand of God was operating through the person of Francesco.

On Sept. 14, 1224, while praying on Mt. Subasio, Jesus appeared to Francesco in the form of a Crucified Seraphim, and immediately he found himself imprinted with *stigmata* of the Lord in his hands, feet, and chest. That caused him great pain for the rest of his life. Francesco died on October 3, 1226; he was forty-four years old. Upon his death, many larks, flying around his tiny chapel, came to bid him the final farewell. Soon, a huge basilica was built to host his mortal remains and Francis became one of the most venerated religious figures in history. Let us remember the second largest city in California would not be called San Francisco if there wasn't San Francesco of Assisi.

Now, let us follow Francesco's footsteps by visiting the major Franciscan sites. Let us have our own *religious rebirth*. "Praised be, my Lord, for Brother Sun and Mother Earth," Francesco used to sing.

Yes, on the morning of Day Nine of our tour, Brother Sun shone and made Mother Earth quite warm. The countryside looked like a huge garden. It was a beautiful and relaxing scene, different from what we had experienced in Milan, Venice, and Florence. Mariano was particularly happy because he had no baggage to load in the bus and his driving time was very short. Going uphill through a grove of olive trees, Mariano took us to Porta Nuova Parking Lot. A long escalator among a wooded park took us to the city's main street; we walked through a massive medieval gate and entered Assisi at Via Borgo Aretino.

Assisi: a medieval street

My enthusiast pilgrims were pleasantly surprised by the old, but neat and picturesque, streets with houses, stores, and restaurants made of grey stone. After going through another old city gate, we came in front of the *Basilica of Santa Chiara* (St. Clare), a real marvel of medieval gothic architecture. That church, reinforced by huge flying buttresses, extends out into the piazza; its facade is made of striped pink and white limestones.

We stopped in *Piazza Santa Chiara* and from there admired the wonderful view of the Umbrian countryside down below. A woman in a long, white dress and white wing, like an angel, invited us to buy her artistic religious souvenirs and wrote for each of us a "message from heaven". Directly below the Piazza, I pointed out a steep hill covered with green olive trees.

Then I said, "This is the exact spot where St. Chiara in 1240 stood and held the Blessed Sacrament in front of the Saracens besieging Assisi. They say those barbarians saw a bright light in the Sacrament, were scared and ran away."

Santa Chiara was a beautiful, young lady born in Assisi from a noble family in 1193. At the age of eighteen, she gave up her possessions, had her blonde hair cut, dressed in a black tunic and a thick veil, and embraced the same lifestyle of St. Francis. She founded the religious Order of Nuns called *Clarisse*. Clare's mother, Ortolana, and her two sisters, Agnes and Beatrice, joined her religious Order. Claire died in Assisi in 1253 at the age of fifty-nine. Recently, she was declared patron saint of television, because, when she was sick and could not attend Mass celebrated miles away, she could see and hear it on the wall of her room.

On the steps of the Basilica, an old woman asked for alms; some of us gave her a few coins. At the entrance door, a custodian made sure everyone was properly dressed and no pictures were taken. As we entered the church, a feeling of mystic holiness and peace overcame us. From behind the main altar, several cloistered nuns sang the morning prayers. It sounded like a choir of angels.

A door to the right of the nave led us into the chapel where the huge crucifix, that spoke to St. Francis, hung from the ceiling. A few people knelt in silent prayer. It felt like if our sins would suddenly become manifest, and the crucifix would speak again, exhorting us to be good people. It was a moving moment that made us happy and frightened at the same time.

Then we descended into the crypt below and stopped in front of a small showroom containing important Franciscan relics, and some personal effects of St. Chiara. Behind a grill, we saw cuttings of her *blonde hair, her cloak, tunic, stockings, sandals, a white shirt, and a gown* she embroidered. Chiara was quite a tall woman. Through those relics, we can imagine what her life must have been like 800 years ago. It was an incredible experience. We descended a few more steps and behind a large glass window we saw *Chiara's body* displayed in a crystal coffin. She was dressed in a dark brownish tunic, a dark veil on her head, and a white collar around her neck. Her face was covered with a yellowish mask made of wax.

A cloistered nun, kneeling by the coffin, handled us a figurine of the saint with a prayer on the back. The nun greeted everybody: "The Lord be with you."

Visitors walked in a single line in front of Clare's coffin; they were silent and overcome by a deep religious feeling. Every heart said a silent prayer. It was a humble, serene, and inspirational sight.

Assisi: St. Clare's tomb

Next, we walked slowly through Corso Mazzini and stopped at the *paternal house* of St. Francis, most of which has been transformed into a church. There is a small square in front of it.

I took the group by two bronze statues, and said, "These represent Saint Francis' parents. Look, the father is holding the clothes Francesco gave him back when he renounced his inheritance, and the mother is showing the chain she broke to free him from house arrest."

In fact, inside the church, we saw the *jail*, a tiny, dark closet where the young Francesco was locked in by his father. Pietro Bernardone was very angry his son refused to help in the family clothing business and was, instead, preaching on the streets of Assisi. Mother Pica secretly freed Francis from that jail during the father's absence. We also saw the *warehouse* where Pietro conducted his daily business.

"One thing was still intact in Francesco's paternal house, *La Porta della Morte* (The door of death). Wealthy families had two doors in their home; one was used for the *living* to go through every day; the other one, a walled-up wooden door, was opened only to carry out the *dead*. A superstitious custom wanted that the living and the dead should not use the same door. The old and eerie wooden door of death can still be seen as it was more than 800 years ago. Even Francis' parents, Pietro Bernardone and Lady Pica, were carried through it."

While walking towards the center of Assisi, someone called my name. It was Signora Francesca, owner of a clothing shop. I had met her during my previous tours. She was very accurate and fast in printing names on the aprons. She invited us into her shop and several ladies bought some personalized embroidered aprons made by her.

We walked a little further and came into *Piazza Comune*, which is the social and political center of Assisi. It is a large and quaint square with medieval buildings, souvenir shops, a bell tower, restaurants, out-door cafés, and an artistic fountain. Walking in this square is like walking back into the long history of Assisi. The restaurants and outdoor cafés in the Piazza were crowded with pilgrims sipping coffee, relishing a gelato, sitting on the steps of the fountain, and watching people pass by. I pointed out to my people the way to a few good restaurants and to the majestic *fortress* on top of the hill.

"What is that old building over there? It looks like a pagan temple," Mario asked.

"That is the church of '*Santa Maria sopra Minerva*'," I explained. "Yes, some two thousand years ago it was a pagan temple dedicated to Venus; later it was consecrated as Christian church. You should go inside and look at the wonderful paintings. Around the altar, you can even see the groove to drain the blood from animals sacrificed to Minerva." Then I said: "It is now 11:00 a.m.; be back to this Piazza at 1:30 p.m., and remember not to eat too much if you want to enjoy another delicious dinner at Villa Verde."

Piazza Comune is a wonderful place to stroll and enjoy the scenic streets in the heart of Assisi. The bells of the tall tower rang every thirty minutes. I sat in a small cafe' and watched people go by. Now and then, small groups of chatting nuns and friars, in their dark brown clothes, crossed the Piazza. Sometimes I imagined seeing the young Francesco talking to his fellow friars. I noticed also the crowd of visitors in Assisi was different from that found in many Italian tourist cities. Here the mood was quiet and reverend with a feeling of peace and inspiration.

At about 1:30 p.m., a man came out of City Hall with a bucket of corn and poured it on the ground of Piazza Comune. Suddenly, many pigeons plummeted out of nowhere and eagerly ate their lunch. They were used to eating in the Piazza at that time.

Just like those birds, at 1:30 p.m. my thirty-five smiling faces also came out of nowhere and regrouped around me. I wanted to find out if their lunch was better than the one the pigeons were having.

I asked Ralph, "What did you eat?"

"Ah, just a little."

"Just a little? He ate a large pizza and drank three glasses of red wine!" his wife objected.

"And what did you eat, Mary?"

"Me? I had only a salad and a small bottle of water without gas."

Paula surprised me with a funny question. "Remo, when are we going to 'Frience'?"

"Frience? There no such place; maybe you mean Firenze?"

"Yes. Yes. That's it. I think so."

"My dear lady, we were in Firenze yesterday and the day before!"

"Oh, I did not know we were there," she replied, with some embarrassment.

Via San Francesco runs from Piazza Comune to the Basilica down the hill. The street is quaint, paved with cobblestones, and lined with beautiful, medieval residences, interesting public buildings from past centuries, souvenir shops, cafés, restaurants, and hotels. Many windows with circlets of wrought iron are filled with red geranium or carnation flowers. The inscription "Pax et Bonum", the favorite greeting of St. Francis, is sculpted above many doors and windows. Along the street, we met many pilgrims; some carried a cross and said prayers. Usually, it takes only ten minutes to walk downhill from Piazza Comune to the Basilica of St. Francis, but we took about forty-five minutes, because people walked slowly and liked browsing inside souvenir shops.

At the end of the street the *Basilica of St. Francis*, built with soft pink and brilliant white stone, appeared as a grandiose and imposing structure. The Basilica consists of three churches built one on top of the other. Those are the Upper Church, the Lower Church, and the Crypt. Built in 1228, right after the death of St. Francis, the Basilica soon became one of the most important places of pilgrimage in the Christian world.

Upon entering the Gothic styled *Upper Church*, one is overcome by a feeling of solemnity and reverence. The walls are entirely covered with the most magnificent frescoes representing twenty-eight scenes of the life and miracles of St. Francis. *Giotto* and *Cimabue* painted the large and impressive frescos, they remain as vivid as when they were painted some 800 years ago. Those are what every art lover longs to see. One needs a few hours to examine all of them. Since tour guides are not allowed to give explanations inside the church, I limited myself to point out the frescoes and whisper a few words to those close to me. I pointed out also the part of the vault that fell and killed a few pilgrims during the earthquake of September 1997. Now the damage has been repaired.

We left the Upper Church from the back apse, descended a narrow and steep staircase and admired the Courtyard of the Friary Sacro Convento. A few more steps down and we entered the dimly lit *Lower Church*. Every inch of the walls and ceiling is covered with medieval paintings depicting scenes from the Bible. Prominent medieval artists made the paintings. It would take hours to study all of them. Those precious paintings make that Basilica one of Italy's most outstanding art museums. One does not need to be Catholic or Christian to appreciate them; one needs to be just a human. In a side chapel, we saw a group of German pilgrims praying and singing. It was an emotional experience.

Halfway down the nave, we descended through a winding staircase and entered a dimly lit small Crypt made of grey stones. There, above a tiny altar, the *mortal remains of Brother Francis* rest in peace in an ancient stone coffin with iron ties. In the four corners of that crypt are entombed Francis' most faithful followers: Ruffino, Angelo, Masseo, and Leone. We found pilgrims ambling around the Saint's tomb, touching it and mumbling prayers. Others sat on wooden pews, praying and meditating. There was an overwhelming sense of peace and calm. One felt a strong divine presence as if St. Francis himself sat in one of those pews and praying with a hood over his head. It was an amazingly moving spiritual experience even to a non-religious person.

It would take a full day to visit the Basilica of St. Francis and discover all its religious and artistic value, but we did it in about an hour and half, which usually is the reasonable time pilgrims can have.

When we exited the Basilica, I said, "Okay, now line up in this beautiful square and let's take a group picture; the short people in front."

A professional photographer took a memorable group picture and delivered copies during our dinner. We walked a little further downhill, passed under an old city gate with a huge medieval wooden door and admired the plain down below strewn with vineyards and olive trees. Mariano's bus came and took us to the majestic *Basilica of Santa Maria degli Angeli* (Saint Mary of the Angels), constructed in 1569. It is a huge building overshadowing the entire area. The basilica was built to shelter some historic Franciscan sites and the vast number of pilgrims. Inside the Basilica, one can find a little chapel, a church within a church, called the *Porziuncola* (The Little Portion, Little Church). That is at least 1200 years old. At the time of St. Francis, it was an abandoned little church in the middle of a wood of oak trees. It was there young Francis met and prayed with his first followers and started the Franciscan religious movement.

Right behind the Porziuncola, we found a very small room called the *Chapel of Transito*. It is a tiny hut originally used as a primitive infirmary for the first friars. St. Francis spent the last hours of his life in there. When he died on the bare ground on Oct. 3, 1226, the people present saw his soul ascend to Heaven in the form of a brilliant star. He was forty-four years old.

Next, we saw the statue of St. Francis with *two live turtle doves* nesting in a basket held by his hands. Those are the descendants of two turtledoves a young man gave Francis as a birthday gift. The saint kept and fed them in his convent. The view of the doves is amazing. At first, one thinks they are dead, but, when they move their eyes, flutter their wings, or fly off, they surprise the visitor.

In front of the "Rose Garden", I asked, "Have you ever seen a rose without thorns?"

"Yes, my wife!" Luigi quickly responded.

I believe Luigi was confused with flowers and people. Tradition holds that on a wintry February night, while St. Francis prayed in his cell, a pretty woman approached him and tried to dissuade him from his pious way of life. Francis chased her away with a crucifix and she disappeared in a big ball of fire. That was the devil himself. To overcome the temptation, Francis rolled his body in a clump of thorny briar. In contact with his body, the bramble bushes immediately bloomed and lost their thorns. The roses without thorns we see today are descendants of that miracle that happened some 800 years ago.

Next to the Rose Garden, we found a sort of cave with an inscription in the middle: "Qui visse San Francesco." (Here lived St. Francis). That is the cell where the saint spent most of his life in prayer and penance.

"Silent Night" is sung during the Christmas season. It was St. Francis who instituted the first *nativity scene* in 1223. He had a live baby representing Jesus, a live woman posing as Mary, and a live man as Joseph. Even the animals, a cow, a donkey, and a sheep were real. They say during Mass, everybody saw a bright light coming from the baby's body.

When we returned to our bus, I said, "If you can sing Sammy Davis' *The Candy Man* song, I will take you to see the real 'Candy Man'."

Immediately, some ladies started singing the song. Therefore, our next stop was at a large *candy factory*. We tasted Grappa, Limoncello and several kinds of chocolate. People bought candies, liqueur, and other goodies. Everyone was tired but very satisfied. A short ride took us back to Villa Verde Hotel where we had another festival of food and entertainment just like the night before.

Assisi: Tomb of St. Francis

CHAPTER 11

MOUNTAINS, HILLS, BEACH!

On the morning of Day Ten of our tour, the peal of the church bells from the nearby Rivotorto Monastery woke us up. As I opened the window, a swarm of festive and screeching swallows flew right in front of my eyes; they were intent in scooping up insects for their breakfast. It was a sunny and mild day; the fields in the valley below were covered with a dew and the top of Mt. Subasio had a white cloud.

When I sat down in the breakfast room a few, cheerful ladies assaulted me with questions, just like those swallows did with their insects.

"Buon Giorno, Remo. Did you sleep well?"

"Did you have nice dreams?"

"May I know how old are you?"

"Are you married?"

"How long have you been married?"

"What is your wife's name?"

"How many children do you have?"

"Why didn't you take your wife with you?"

"Are we going to the beach today?"

"Ah, ah, you are gaining weight!"

It seemed those women were going to give me a test about my private life. Quickly, I put an end to the questions by asking: "Ladies, do you know what breakfast means? It means you *break* your *fast*. You fast during the night and you break it in the morning; it is a short overnight fast!"

The baggage was loaded on the bus, the staff at Villa Verde was thanked, the morning prayer was said and another enjoyable journey began.

"How long is it to the next hotel?" Mary asked.

"It will be almost four hours, but we will take breaks along the way."

"Four hours on the bus? Impossible!" Mary protested.

"My lady, would you prefer to walk instead? This is a very special day, because you will discover the real Italian life without walking. Just sit in your royal throne and enjoy the beautiful scenery."

We drove by the picturesque hill town of Spello with its intact, medieval walls draped around the historic center like a necklace. A plump young nun led a group of school children; she held the hand of the child in the front. The youngsters wore blue uniforms with a white collar and a large blue bow tie. The children sang: "La gallina bianca con le gambe rosse…" (The white chicken with red legs…). That was a song I had not heard since I was a child. It gave me goosebumps and brought back wonderful memories.

On the outskirt of Foligno, we took highway 77 and headed east to the Adriatic Sea. We had to cross the Appennini Mountains. Soon the plain ended and a scenic drive began; we climbed through a winding country road. Long rows of green olive trees, pencil pines, and grape vines formed a spectacular landscape down below. A handful of stone houses and tiny villages perched on hill top could be seen here and there. They had remained unchanged for centuries. It was an idyllic setting. A few ladies in the back of the bus sang, "Country road, take me home…" like John Denver.

Our bus kept on climbing and went through a couple of villages. Mariano honked any time he made a sharp turn in the slopes of the mountain. Further up there were no more olive trees, only chestnut and oak trees.

"What kind of animal live in these woods?" Sandra asked.

"Lions, tigers, bears…" I answered with a grin.

Immediately, all the women reacted: "Lions, tigers, and bears. Oh, my!" Were we going to see "The Wizard of Oz"? Spirits were high and the joking continued when on the left side of the mountain, we saw a very old hermitage under a large cracked rock.

"How does the hermit get up there? There is no road." Peter wondered.

"Ah, I bet he is watching some dirty movie on TV. Look, he's got electric power!" Joe remarked. "That is the hermitage of San Giacomo, nestled high up among rocky crags. It has been there for the past 800 years as a place of pilgrimage. The hermitage can be reached by climbing on foot to a steep uphill."

We took our first coffee break in Colfiorito, a neat village with stone houses and narrow streets. The village still shows some damage from the 1997 earthquake. We parked the bus in the town's square and walked to Stella Alpina, the only coffee shop in town. The dining room, the ceiling beams, window frames, tables, and chairs were all made of old oak wood. Inside, there were three elderly men playing cards and a woman buying ricotta, fresh bread, green beans, and a gelato (ice cream) for her child.

Ennio, the young attendant, greeted us with a warm "Buon Giorno," but when he realized we spoke another language, he immediately called his sister Rosalia, who proudly spoke some English. Soon, grandfather Donato joined the company; he enthusiastically told us about his trip to Jessup, PA, where he had a cousin.

We occupied the entire rustic dining room. There was a display of tempting homemade pastries and most of us had *cannoli* and fresh aromatic coffee. When Luciano, a local shepherd, came in and asked for a "panino" and a glass of red wine, Rosalia prepared for him an appetizing sandwich with olive oil, mozzarella cheese, prosciutto (ham), and tomato. That made our mouths water, and Rosalia sold us many panini. Peter, John, and a few other men in our group also had a glass of wine. Our hosts made us feel at home and when we left Ennio, Rosalia, and Donato came by the bus to wish us "Buon Viaggio" (Happy Trip). Our stop at Stella Alpina was a pleasant experience.

On the road again, we traveled through more idyllic countryside. In fact, along the way we found a large flock of sheep crossing the road. The shepherd, a man in the early fifties, wore a brown cone hat with a peacock feather, a short beard, dark trousers, a reddish checkered shirt, a greenish wool jacket, and a pair of worn boots. He carried a stick in his right hand, an old umbrella and a tottered bag hanging from his back. When he saw our bus approaching, he became nervous because several sheep wandered about, and others stood right in the middle of the road. Two white sheepdogs helped the shepherd to keep order in the flock, but some sheep did not obey. We stopped the bus and some of us jumped off, took pictures, and enjoyed the scene. Tony and Paul helped the shepherd to bring the stray sheep back to the flock. Luisa posed while petting a lamb, and then she gave the shepherd a large chocolate bar. He kissed her hand, gave her a small *pecorino cheese*, and kept on saying:

"Grazie, Grazie, Bella Signora!"

We only traveled about two more miles when we had to stop the bus again. A huge white animal stood defiantly in the middle of the country road.

"The holy cow! The holy cow!" Linda yelled.

Actually, it was a bull. He looked at us but did not budge. After a while, I got off the bus, walked over to the bull, and whispered something into his ear. Immediately, the bull cleared the road and ran up the hill.

"How did you get him to move? What did you tell him?" everyone wanted to know.

I told him: "Listen, you big, fat bull, these are Americans and they just crushed your cousin's balls in Milan. You better move or else!" Everyone applauded that explanation.

As in many Italian country roads, along highway 77 we saw a few *cappelline*. Those are very small shrines on the side of the road; they usually contain in a glass frame a picture of the Virgin Mary or a crucifix. Those shrines were built in the olden times when people walked to town. They invite travelers to pause and perform some act of devotion. In fact, most passers-by remove their hat, make the sign of cross, and say a silent prayer; sometimes they bring a flower and continue their way. Those shrines still bear witness to people's religious devotion and are valuable examples of folk art, culture, and traditions of past generations.

When we reached the top of the mountain, we drove through the Colfiorito Plateau, an upland plain of undulated landscape surrounded by mountain peaks. The plateau is used for cultivation of *patate rosse* (red potatoes), fodder, lentils, *ceci* (chick peas), garlic, and onions. In fact, as we drove along the road, we saw a few tractors and pick-up trucks laden with bags of red potatoes and other things. By the tractors and small trucks, one can always see a man or a woman sitting in a chair under a large umbrella. The *patate rosse* are sold all over Italy because they have a special taste and used mostly to make delicious "gnocchi" and other pasta items.

Rose asked, "Could we stop? I would like to buy some lentils and cook them for New Year's Day, as my grandmother used to do. They bring good luck for the entire year."

On the back of a pick-up truck, we saw a pretty farmer woman smiling and selling red potatoes. She had a dark blue dress, a reddish apron, and long, black hair tied with a red headscarf.

Upon seeing her, Mario sighed: "Wow, look at that! Let us stop. I want a picture with her."

We stopped. A few people got off the bus; Rose got her lentils and Mario had a picture with that farmer woman, who proudly posed as if she was selling him a bundle of garlic. Mario thanked her with a kiss on the cheek.

Shortly after that, the highway descended into a wooded hill and went right through what was once the courtyard of the mighty *Serravalle Castle*. The Duc of Varano resided there and had parties and good life some 800 years ago. Today, only a dilapidated tower and a few walls and ramparts remain. A plaque by a small amount of ruins reads:

"Ruderi della ponderosa fortezza che proteggeva il Ducato dei Varano". (Ruins of the powerful fortress that protected the Dukedom of the Varano).

When we approached the town of Muccia, we passed by a small cemetery surrounded by a wall. Above the entrance door, a large inscription read:

"Qui per sempre posano affetti, vanita', speranze" (Here, forever rest affections, vanity, hopes).

I explained that Italian cemeteries, big or small, are well-kept and very few people are buried in the ground. Most families have a tiny chapel where they bury their loved ones.

Soon, Mariano had to stop again. There was a funeral procession with at least fifty people walking in the middle of the road. It was preceded by a priest and a band playing funeral music. Following the band, four men carried a casket on their shoulders. Relatives and friends, all dressed in black, walked right behind the casket. They were sobbing. A crowd followed them. The women recited the rosary, and the men walked silently. All of them looked at us with curiosity. Tour busses were a rare sight in those mountain villages.

Just before the entrance to the town of Serravalle, we could see farms with horses and cows grazing freely in the green pastures. Ducks, chickens, turkeys, and rabbits shared a large yard and lived peacefully together. An old woman with a bucket of grain was surrounded by many chickens. We waved at her and she waved back while a chicken tried to climb to the rim of her bucket.

As the road continued through the town of Serravalle, it became so narrow the traffic was reduced to one way and controlled by a stoplight. Our bus stopped right by an open space where we saw a large vegetable garden. There were rows of tomatoes, peppers, green beans, artichokes, eggplants, a few fig trees, and an apple tree. Along the house was a large pile of winter firewood. A man with a straw hat tilled the ground with a hoe.

"Which Italian regions have you seen by now?" I asked.

Some named one or two, but Mary named all of them: Piemonte, Lombardia, Veneto, Emilia, Tuscana, and Umbria.

"Brava! And now we are in the region called *Marche*. Now, I have a surprise for you: we are going to have lunch in a real country restaurant."

We drove through the small village of Pieve and arrived at a large farmhouse called "Agriturismo Terra della Sibilla". I had made reservation; they were waiting for us. The tables were set in a large open barn. Immediately, the owner, Signora Adelina, greeted us and introduced her staff. We explored the grounds, petted a goat and two cats, and then sat down for another festival of food. The antipasto was a local specialty called "insalata di funghi" (mushroom salad). For the main course, they served homemade "gnocchi" with duck sauce. Then we had a tender steak of "cinghiale" (wild boar) with oven cooked apples, potatoes, and asparagus. A heavenly dessert of ricotta with honey and nuts was lip-licking-good. We had all wine, water, and coffee we wanted. We were treated like royalties and the price was very modest.

After that delicious lunch, we returned to the main road. The mountains yielded to the hills. In the valleys below we could see cows and sheep peacefully grazing. Horses were nonchalantly walking inside an area enclosed with a white fence. There were fields strewn with old farm houses, vineyards, and olive orchards. The grapes were ready to be harvested, but the olives were still green. That pastoral scene reminded me of another delightful story.

I asked, "Do you remember when farmers had machines that made *square* bales of hay?"

"Yes, I certainly do," a few men replied.

"But now the new machines make only *round bales*. Right?"

"Right. So what?"

"Well, when they made those round bales, the Italian cows went on a hunger strike. Do you know why?"

"No. Why?"

"Because they could no longer have a *square meal*!"

Everybody laughed. Some women said, "You are such a comedian. Where do you get your jokes?"

We drove by the medieval town of Tolentino, and after that the country road turned into a modern highway with two lanes in each direction. The bus increased speed and my happy travelers, overcome by the effects of wine at the Agriturismo, dozed.

About forty-five minutes later, I picked up the microphone and chanted: "Do you see what I see? I see the sea!" As my thirty-five sleeping fellows opened their eyes, I said, "I see you are tired, but try not to miss the fantastic, blue coast of the Adriatic Sea. Sleep with your left eye and look with your right eye!"

Those who fought the fatigue were rewarded with unforgettable views: on our left side, there were picturesque towns on top of hills; on the right, by the beach, modern villages followed one another. In summer, sunbathers invade those villages. Although it was late September, several people enjoyed the "spiaggia" (beach). On the horizon, the deep blue sea seemed to meet the pale blue sky.

At the seaside resort town of Civitanova, we took the Autostrada (Freeway) A14 and headed north for about twenty minutes. Then, on the left side, a picturesque town on top of a hill appeared like a mirage. In the center of the town, we could see a huge building resembling a fortress. That is the *Santa Casa* (The Holy House) of *Loreto,* one of the most revered shrines of Christianity.

According to tradition, the Santa Casa is the house where the Virgin Mary was born, grew up, and received the annunciation in Nazareth. Later, the house was converted into a church by the first Christians. The tradition also says when, in 1294, the Turks threatened to destroy it, the angels carried the little house to the town called *Loreto;* others claim the Crusaders brought it there. Archeological evidence tells the tiny house certainly did not originate in Italy because the stones, bricks, and dirt used in the construction cannot be found in Loreto or anywhere in Italy, but they are made of the same limestone elements found in the ground of Nazareth. Moreover, the humble, little dwelling has no foundation and seems to have been laid on the hill of Loreto like a box. Furthermore, the foundation left behind in Nazareth was of the same dimensions as the lowest part of the house that mysteriously appeared in Loreto.

To protect that precious home, its rough walls have been cased in with rich sculptured marble and that, in turn, is enclosed in a magnificent Basilica. The Santa Casa has been the scene of many miraculous cures and it draws people from all over the world. In the marble around the external wall of that little house, one can see the shallow grooves made by the pilgrims circling the shrine on their knees.

In the large square in front the Santa Casa, we watched a group of pilgrims entering the shrine. Their leader had a banner with the inscription: "Parrocchia S. Anna. Campobasso" (St. Anna Parish. Campobasso, a city in central Italy).

Those pilgrims sang the popular religious chant "Mira al tuo popolo, Oh Bella Signora..." (Look at your people, oh, Beautiful Lady). We followed them and accessed the Basilica; then we timidly entered that tiny one room house where the Holy Family lived, worked, ate, and slept! The scene was overwhelming.

Loreto: the Holy House

After visiting the shrine, I gave some free time for lunch and souvenir shopping. Then we rode south, along the Adriatic coast. When we entered the *Abruzzo* region, people with family roots there, including myself, shouted for joy.

"How far is it to the hotel?" Rose asked.

"Rose, we are closer now than when we left this morning," I answered with a snicker.

"Well, we better be!" she commented.

Abruzzo is in central Italy and stretches from the heart of the Appennini to the Adriatic Sea. Its inhabitants are called "Abruzzesi" and are nicknamed "forti e gentili" (strong and gentle). The region is mostly mountainous and hilly. The main cities are L'Aquila, Chieti, Teramo, and Pescara. Many Italian-Americans have family roots in that area.

Our next stop was at *Peppino's Frantoio* (Oil Mill) in Giulianova. We saw how olives are crushed and made into oil. Peppino is also great at making a special soap with his oil. I had taken another group there in June and when Peppino saw me in September he asked me to translate a letter he had received from Nick, a gentleman in my previous tour. The letter praised the extraordinary quality of the soap Nick had bought at that Frantoio. The soap was made with olive oil and other local aromatic ingredients. The letter concluded: "I gave one soap bar to my girlfriend Angelina and within a few days her skin became so soft and beautiful that I kiss her much more often..."

Imagine: when my people heard that, Peppino sold all the magic soap he had available that day. He received hugs from all the ladies in the group! We checked into the modern *Hermitage Hotel* at about 5:00 p.m. That four-star hotel is located right on the sandy beach, near Pescara. All rooms had a view of the sea. Surprise: within twenty minutes everybody was in the water or walking on the beach.

In the towns near the sea they serve delicious fresh fish; in fact, that evening for dinner we had a whole *pesce trota* (trout fish) with lemon, parsley, rosemary, and butter.

"I cannot eat it. Look at those big open eyes staring at me! They are scary! Why don't they cut the fish's head?" Ann protested.

Waiter Massimo took her dish to the kitchen, chopped off the head, and served it to Ann again.

"No! Look at that poor decapitated fish. I still cannot eat it! Take it away, please take it away!" she screamed again. She had suddenly become allergic to fish.

Massimo was kind enough to serve her a nice dish of mozzarella cheese with prosciutto and salad.

Paul and Mary were the last ones to come to the dining room. Since all seats were taken, the waiter prepared an additional table for them and placed two bottles of wine on it, red and white. After a while, we noticed those two were getting rather romantic.

"Look at the honeymooners!" I said.

Yes, they drank both bottles of wine and the effect showed. Mary kept laughing, and her mood became contagious; laughter spread throughout the rest of the group. After dinner, Paul and Mary, holding hands, came by the bar and made us laugh even more. Then they disappeared on the sandy beach, under the dim moonlight. The rest of the group gathered around a piano, where Betty played some music and made us dance.

Our Hermitage Hotel

CHAPTER 12

GOING ON A SENTIMENTAL JOURNEY

The next morning, just as the sun peaked over the sea, Karen Gentile came downstairs singing:

"I am going to take my sentimental journey!"

Luigi echoed: "This is the day the Lord has made. Alleluia!"

They were so happy because their dream was coming true: they were going to see the town from which their grandparents came. In fact, that was the main reason they came on the tour.

Although the Italian explorer Cristoforo Colombo (Christopher Columbus) discovered America in 1492, it wasn't until early 1900s many Italians immigrated to the new continent. Most of them came from central and southern Italy. They left behind parents, affections, brothers, sisters, houses, and friends. They were young, hardworking, and determined to build a better future in the land of opportunities. As time passed, most of them never had the opportunity of returning to Italy. Their children learned English and could barely speak Italian. Unfortunately, soon all contacts with the *old country* were lost. However, the children of those immigrants always kept in their heart the desire of visiting the dear, little town where their folks originated, see the old house they lived in, walk on the same roads they walked, look at the same mountains, eat the same food, and meet their living relatives.

Today, with the improved economy and faster means of traveling, many Italian-Americans are making that dream come true.

In Milan, Venice, Florence and Assisi my *Abruzzesi* Karen, Mario, Luigi, and Ralph had seen numerous artistic wonders made by the world's greatest artists. There was nothing like that in Abruzzo. Yet, that day they were emotionally overwhelmed. Why? Because they were going to see the small town and the modest house where their grandparents were born and grew up. They were going to meet relatives, walk on the same cobblestone streets their forefathers walked, and pray in the beautiful church they attended. A visit to the cemetery was also in the plan. For Karen, Mario, Luigi, and Ralph that small town was the most beautiful place on Earth; that modest house was the greatest museum and their grandparents were the greatest artists that ever lived!

The region of Abruzzo is the most mountainous area of the Appennini. The *Gran Sasso* and *Maiella,* both about 10,000 feet high, are the tallest peaks. Snow can be seen atop there from late September to late June. From the mountains to the sea, there are about forty miles of rolling hills covered with olive trees, fig trees, vineyards, and fields of wheat.

Although Abruzzo is one of the most beautiful regions of Italy, until recently it was mostly known as *Terra dei pastori* (shepherds' land) with plenty of silent valleys and stone clad medieval hilltop towns. Even nowadays, Abruzzo is off the beaten path and not on the list of places to be visited by foreign tourists. But, when the Italian-Americans visit that area, they wonder why their grandparents left that wonderful place. The answer given by Luigi's uncle says it all:

"Caro Nipote, tuo nonno parti' perche' aveva lo stomaco vuoto." (Dear Nephew, your grandfather left because he had an empty stomach).

In the morning of Day Eleven of our tour, the sunrise was glorious. About half of the group chose to stay at Hermitage Hotel and enjoy the beautiful sandy beach. Since I had only eighteen people left, Mariano came with a mini-bus, which was easier to operate through the narrow-winding country roads of Abruzzo.

Mario had family roots in *Palena*, a small town in the Province of Chieti, on the eastern slope of Mt. Maiella. That was out of our way and it was impossible for me to take him there that same day. No problem! I had arranged with a friend of mine to take Mario and his wife to Palena.

"When you get to Palena," I told Mario, "tell people you are a friend of Perry Como. All doors will then open to you."

Perry Como also has family roots in the town of Palena.

Luigi De Angelis' grandparents came from *Barisciano*, a town near the city of L'Aquila. They settled in Bellaire, Ohio. About a month before leaving for Italy, I contacted in Barisciano few families with that last name. I explained who Luigi's grandparents were and inquired if he had any living relatives there. Giuseppe De Angelis responded and assured he was indeed a close relative. We dropped Luigi and his wife in the town of Popoli and Giuseppe picked them up. Their encounter was very emotional.

We continued along the foot of Mt. Maiella and then through the Sulmona Valley. As the bus went under a low bridge, I said, jokingly, "Watch your head! Duck in so the bus can make it!"

Some people really lowered their head! They enjoyed humoring me. The Sulmona Valley is an oval plain about twenty-five miles long, surrounded by high mountains. At the beginning of last century, many young men and women left that valley and went to America. In particular, the towns of Pettorano, Introdacqua, Pratola, Bugnara, Rocca Pia, Corfinio, Popoli, Pacentro, and Collepietro saw a massive exodus. In America, most of them settled in Ohio (Steubenville, Mingo Junction, Columbus), in West Virginia (Weirton, Follansbee, Wellsburg), and in the Pittsburgh, PA, area.

Karen Gentile's *Nonno* (grandfather), Peppino Gentile, left Pettorano in 1923 and settled in Pittsburgh. Over the years, all contacts between Peppino and his people in Pettorano went lost. Karen wasn't even sure she still had any living relatives there. To facilitate identifying them, she brought many pictures of the Gentile families in America.

We bypassed the city of Sulmona and continued south on State Route 17. Soon the town of Pettorano appeared from afar. It looked like a very picturesque town on a steep hilltop, at the foot of Mt. Genzana. The red-roofed houses, set in tiers, were built one on top of the other. On the highest point, there was a tall and medieval castle overlooking the entire town and valley below.

Mariano slowed the bus and a few pictures were taken. We left the main road, passed a narrow bridge over the Gizio River, and drove into a wooded area for about half mile. We noticed a couple of women washing clothes on the ledge of a rock alongside the Gizio. A road sign warned to beware of bears. In fact, later we were told some bears do come down the mountain in summer and hibernate in winter. When we saw the road sign *Pettorano*, Karen's heart filled with emotion. The bus stopped, she practically jumped out and stood by the sign to have pictures taken. When we reached the first houses of the town, an elderly woman, with a dark blue dress and a white apron waved at us. Immediately, we waved back. We parked the bus in the small St. Nicola Square, at the bottom of the town. Some people went for a coffee in a little bar.

I asked two elderly men sitting outside the bar: "Scusate, dov'e' la piazza principale?" (Excuse me, where is main square?)

"Su, su. Sempre su." (Up, up. Always up), they responded pointing out the top of the town.

My entire crew of sixteen people was anxious to see life in that small mountain town. Karen followed me and the others followed her. Excitement filled the air and we laughed and talked as we walked to downtown Pettorano. The only way to go *downtown* Pettorano is to walk *uptown*!

While strolling through the town we felt like we were going back in time to the Middle Ages. The solid stone houses and cobblestone streets have been there for centuries. Main Street is narrow, steep, paved with cobblestones, and interrupted by large stepping stones. Along the street, we encountered short and narrow alleys, steep external staircases, and meandering pathways. We noticed all first-floor windows have protective wrought iron bars and the entire town maintains an intact medieval layout. Obviously, no cars can access those narrow streets.

A visitor might assume the town is empty. That emptiness is better felt if one thinks of the massive emigration that left Pettorano with only 1,300 inhabitants. Yet, old Pettorano does not mean neglected Pettorano. The streets are kept clean; pots of geraniums and carnations could be seen in many windows, in balconies and in the exterior staircases. People have all the modern comforts inside their homes. A few small, noble patrician palaces, with artistic coat of arms etched in stone archways reminded us Pettorano was once a pulsating town of 5,000 inhabitants.

Today, most men in that town work as farmers, shepherds, woodcutters, stone masons, stone carvers, tailors, goldsmiths, copper and wrought iron, and basket makers. The women are housewives and excellent weavers; they make colorful lace shawls, beautiful woolen blankets, table clothes, and they prepare delicious polenta in winter.

Since we were a noisy bunch on the street, a few curious women looked at us from their window, while others peeked from the front door. A woman, knitting by her doorway was completely surprised to see us; she kept on staring at us for a longtime. Through an open door and a dim smoke, we could see and hear the village smith hammering some metal on an anvil. An old shoemaker repaired boots outside his shop; when he saw us, he laid down his tools and kept on looking at us. A pretty, young woman hummed a song while hanging a few dresses on a clothes line. An elderly man, wearing a little round hat and wide pants, came down the street leading a mule loaded with firewood; the mule sent a few brays now and then. Another old man passed by us; he held a cane and led a flock of about ten sheep. We waved and greeted everyone very warmly, but they responded only with a cold *Buon Giorno* and kept on looking at us with suspicion. They had the impression we were just a bunch of foreigners invading their town. Were we invaders or tourists? Except for a few Italian-Americans, no tourist ever visits that remote mountain town!

Pettorano

After an exhausting climb, we finally arrived to the small, old, and charming *Piazza Zannelli,* the town's main square. *Bar Torchio* had a few outside tables and a pleasant view of the valley. (Remember: bar = coffee shop). About ten elder men were attentively playing cards. They too stopped playing and looked at us with much curiosity, without saying a word. There I used my usual *trick* to find relatives.

"Buon Giorno a tutti!" (Good morning, everybody), I warmly greeted. "This lady is American, but her Nonno *Peppino Gentile* was from here. Do you know any Gentile family in town?"

Their cold curiosity immediately turned into a warm friendship. "Gentile? I am Gabriele Gentile!" said a well-built man. He was in his early seventies, had a mustache and wore a pointed straw hat and a greenish Alpine jacket.

I explained who Peppino was, but Gabriele could not connect with him. He kindly walked us to the house of Domenico Gentile who had spent a couple of years in Steubenville, Ohio. Domenico was neither related to Karen.

Finally, we learned that years earlier *Giovanni Gentile* had visitors from America. Gabriele kindly and proudly walked with us to the top of the town and called Giovanni, an eighty-year-old man.

"Chi e'?" (Who is it?) said a voice from inside the house.

"Questi sono americani. Credo che sono parenti con te." (These are Americans. I believe they are related to you).

Giovanni came to the door. He wore brown pants and a light tan sweater; he smoked an old, curved pipe. For a few seconds, he remained pensive and then he smiled and asked:

"Did you know my late brother Pasquale Gentile in Pittsburgh?"

"Pasquale Gentile? Yes! He was my father's cousin! So, your father and my grandfather were brothers! Oh, my God!" shouted Karen with a trembling voice. Giovanni and Karen hugged each other for a long-time. Tears filled their eyes and we could barely hold back ours.

Giovanni invited us inside and called his wife, Carmela, and daughter-in-law, Lucia. Immediately, Carmela ran to her bedroom and put on a long colorful apron. She hugged Karen and filled the table with cookies, grapes, figs, and soft drinks. Giovanni ran to the cellar and returned with two big bottles of red wine made with his grapes. Lucia was in her forties; she had a navy-blue skirt, an ivory button blouse and a black knitted vest. She was busy helping Carmela. Including Mariano and myself, we were eighteen guests crammed into Giovanni's little dining room. Our hosts opened their home and heart to us.

I had little chance to taste the goodies on the table, because Karen and Giovanni talked for a long time and I was busy translating everything they said. Karen placed on the table many photos of the Gentile family in America. Pointing out to each picture, she gave the name of each person and explained how they were related to her. Carmela searched through her bundle of pictures and found one showing

Karen's grandparents and her father Nicola, when he was a little boy. The back of that picture read "Pittsburgh 1927". There were so many pictures I became confused as to who was who.

Karen's husband, Tony, reminded her to give the Gentile family the token gift she had brought for them. Immediately, she pulled a small Statue of Liberty out of her purse, kissed it and gave it to Carmela. Then, they exchanged addresses, telephone numbers, and promised to keep the contact alive.

Vincenzo, Giovanni's son, was in the field, repairing a wooden shelter for his sheep. When he learned of the unexpected visit, he rushed home and joined the family's happiness. He felt uneasy and apologized for wearing work clothes. He wore old boots, dark pants, a checkered shirt, and a large red handkerchief around his neck. Karen and Tony put him at easy when they hugged him warmly.

Pierino, Giovanni's grandson, was about seven years old. When he returned from school and found his house invaded by people talking a funny language, he sat silently in a corner and kept on looking at us. He had never been exposed to people speaking another language. Then, suddenly, he said (in Italian, of course): "Nonno (grandpa), what is wrong with these people? Let us take them to my dentist. He will fix their mouth and they will talk normal!"

Everyone laughed. Karen gave Pierino a big hug and a few chocolate bars.

After a while, most of the people in our group thanked Giovanni, walked outside, and stopped at Bar Torchio; they tried to engage in a conversation with the locals. Knowing we were guests of Giovanni Gentile, the men immediately became everybody's friend.

One of them said: "When you go back to America, go to see my cousin Arturo in San Diego. Tell him you saw me, Michele."

"Say hi to my *Cumpare* (friend) Paolo in San Luigi (St. Louis)," said another man.

While Carmela and Lucia prepared a delicious quick lunch, Giovanni and Karen sat on a couch next to each other and kept on looking at the family pictures and exchanging all the information they could re-member. Karen told all she knew about her family.

"My Nonno Peppino and my Nonna Grazietta," she explained, "were married in Pettorano in 1917. He attended sheep and she was a housewife. When their friend Armando, a shoemaker in Bridgeport, PA, sponsored them, the young couple left for America in 1923. My nonno left a sister and a brother in Pettorano and my nonna had a brother and two sisters. My grandparents went to America with their three-year-old daughter, Teresa. Later, they had two more children, Nicola and Carlo. Nonno Peppino worked in a steel mill in Pitts-burgh for thirty-two years. He purchased a house with a large yard. My nonna ran a boarding house for a few newly arrived Italian im-migrants. My grandparents made their own pasta and bread and had a large garden where they grew all kinds of vegetables. My nonno took particular care of his grapevines and a few fig trees. He loved playing cards and bocce, drinking wine, and singing Italian songs with his friends. For many years, my grandparents kept in touch with their parents in Pettorano. They sent some money and packages with clothes and shoes to help during the war. My grandparents never had the chance to go back to see their people in Pettorano. Nonno Pep-pino died in 1948 and Nonna Grazietta in 1963. After their death, my father and his siblings could not speak Italian and thus all contact with the relatives in Pettorano went lost. Later, we didn't even know if we had any family in there."

Karen continued, "Aunt Teresa married a man from Introdacqua, had four children, and died in 2003. Uncle Carlo was an engineer; he achieved success by building roads and bridges in West Pennsylvania. Carlo had five children and died in 2008. My father, Nicola, worked with his father in a steel mill, but later opened a restaurant in the Bloomfield, Pittsburgh area. They were quite successful and all Ital-ian-Americans their place. My parents had two children, Mary and my-self. Mary is a retired school teacher. I married Tony Barbieri, a dentist. I recently retired as a nurse. We have two children, Angela and Betty.

Angela is married and has one child, Joe. Betty has Mary and Grace. I will try to have my family come to Pettorano next year." Karen showed Giovanni pictures of all her family and relatives in America.

Giovanni told the history of his own family. It was a short history since he lived all the time in the same house and took care of his small farm in the outskirt of Pettorano. He remembered getting letters and clothes from some relatives in America. Giovanni had two sons, Mario and Vincenzo. Mario died in North Africa during World War II and Vincenzo worked on the farm with his father. Pierino was the only grandson to delight Nonno Giovanni.

While the two kept on talking, Carmela and Lucia prepared a quick lunch. They placed on the table a large tray of hot, smoking pasta, a dish of sausage, salad, bread, wine, and coffee. Carmela apologized for the meager meal; she said she would have prepared a better one if she knew of the visit. Giovanni said a short thanksgiving prayer and then shouted "Buon Appetito, Cara Cugina." (Have a good meal, dear cousin!). The food was delicious; everything was homemade. Karen insisted the food tasted just like the one her Nonna Grazietta used to prepare. Carmela served eight guests, since a few other people had left and were having lunch at Bar Torchio. Soon after a few other people rushed to Giovanni's house and enthusiastically greeted their American "parenti" (relatives).

Giovanni wished Karen could stay for a few days, but time did not allow. As a farewell gift, he gave her a small bag of *fave* (fava beans) to symbolize the precious seeds for all family members in Pittsburgh. Then, Giovanni, Carmela, Vincenzo, and Lucia walked Karen to a nearby old stone house.

"This is where all Gentile people were born, including your Nonno Peppino," said Giovanni.

Karen kissed the wall of the old house, took pictures, and cried. She removed a little stone from the wall and picked a carnation flower from a pot. "These are my most precious souvenirs," she said with tears in her eyes.

We walked a little further up the hill and stopped in front of the medieval parish church *Santa Maria*. An old woman came down the steps; she wore a long, dark, pleated skirt and a long and a red apron; a white shawl covered her head and shoulders. Many older women in Pettorano pride themselves wearing a traditional costume when going to church.

On the left side of the church wall we saw an artistic plaque honoring the young soldiers of Pettorano who died during World War II. There were two Gentile; one was Mario, Giovanni's son.

We entered Santa Maria Church where Nonno Peppino and Nonna Grazietta were married in 1917. Karen knelt in front of the main altar and cried there too. The parish priest, Padre Raffaele, came and gave us a brief history of the church; then he wrote a birth and a marriage certificate of Karen's grandparents. She made a little donation in their memory.

The news of our presence quickly spread in town. As we came out of the church, we found about fifteen people anxiously waiting for us. Some were Karen's distant relatives, some wanted us to bring greetings to their relatives in the States, and others came just to see Americans. Everybody in Pettorano had some relative in America. I was very busy, translating everything people said.

Giovanni and his family walked us down through the narrow street until we arrived at our bus. They kept saying:

"Che bella sorpresa! Grazie! Dio vi benedica." (What a wonderful surprise. Thanks. May God bless you).

Karen hugged Giovanni and his family. She was so moved and crying, she could barely talk. Some of our ladies took her by the arm. Karen kept on saying: "Oh, my God! I cannot believe this! This is the highlight of my tour. I must come back with my children." Later, Karen told us: "In seeing my relatives in Pettorano, I was overpowered by the pain my grandparents felt when they left their own parents, relatives, and friends forever. At the same time, I was overcome by the joy of finally reuniting with my family. I feel like I belong to Pettorano."

We left at about 2:00 p.m.

Meeting Relatives

We drove back a few miles and, by Sulmona, took the country road 487 going to *Pacentro*. That is another medieval town atop a hill, at the western foot of the mighty Maiella mountain. Pacentro is slightly larger than Pettorano. Like all mountain towns in the Sulmona Valley, Pacentro has narrow and old cobblestone streets, stone houses, pots of flowers in many windows, and a few medieval churches. The impressive 14th century Cantelmo Castle looms over the town. *Ralph Mancini* had family roots in that town.

We arrived to Pacentro when most people were having their afternoon siesta. At Piazza Santa Maria, only a couple of men sat outside a bar. I asked if they knew any Mancini family. Within minutes, Ralph was in the arms of relatives he had never met. Our visit there was an exact repetition of our experience with the Gentile Family; the only difference was Ralph had less time to spend with his relatives. There were hugs, food, wine, and pictures. Ralph saw the house of his grandfather. He also wanted to see the 15th century parish church of Santa Maria della Misericordia, but it was closed. He kissed the walls of the church and took many pictures.

A young lady from a window asked, "Do you know the singer Madonna? I am related to her." Madonna's paternal grandparents came from Pacentro. We said good-bye to Pacentro at about 5:00 p.m.

During the previous days, we always had dinner in the hotel, but that evening I wanted to give the group a special treat in a country restaurant. From Pacentro, we returned to our hotel and picked up the rest of the group. Then, we drove to my town *Pianella*. On the way, we could see the neatly manicured country side strewn with vineyards and olive trees. A sign at the entrance of town said: "Benvenuti nella Citta' dell'olio" (Welcome to the city of oil). Yes, my town is famous for its *extra virgin olive oil*.

"If you are virgin, how much more virgin can you be?" asked Marc with an impertinent voice.

"Well, that may apply to you, but not to olives!" I rebutted.

We passed through the center of Pianella and I asked everybody to look for my statue on the square. Then, "There it is!" I shouted jokingly. Everyone saw a statue, but no, it was not me; it was the statue of an old war hero. "That is not fair! They have replaced me. I will complain to the mayor!" I protested. People shook their heads and smiled.

On the outskirts of town, we passed by my paternal stone house with green shutters. Some ladies took pictures of it. Soon after, I told Mariano, "Turn right, where that car is coming from." We arrived at the country restaurant called *Vecchio Silos* (Old Silos). My ninety-eight-year-old *Mamma Lucia*, cousin *Gabriele* and cousin *Gina* were outside, anxiously waiting for us. After I hugged my mother and cousins, everybody did the same. A few men walked by a fig tree and ate fresh figs, while others went for a picture under an olive tree.

The large dining room was ready for us. We sat down and were promptly served a dish of *antipasto* with *bruschetta*, cheese, prosciutto, salami, olives, pickled artichokes, and other savory things. Then, three waiters came out with a big terracotta pot containing something dark, golden, boiling, and smoking. Ah, that was *Pasta e Fagioli* (pasta and beans), the specialty of the house! In olden times, it was considered a *Poor Man's Meal,* but today it is a favorite dish sought by everyone. It is so tasty you want more; in fact, some men ate three bowls, and Tony bragged he ate four!

In the meanwhile, DJ Lorenzo played Italian folk music. A few couples got up and danced; before long, others joined them and excitement was on everybody's face. Chef-owner, Fernando, and his mother, Rosaria, were busy cooking in the kitchen. Fernando's sister Elisabetta helped the waiters.

Before the night ended, my thirty-five diners became a wound-up group. Generous amount of red and white wine was working on them. Next, we had two kinds of spaghetti with delicious sauce, fried chicken, sausage, roasted potatoes, salad, grapes, cake, coffee, champagne, and many other exquisite treats. Cousin Gabriele had for us a basket of fresh figs he had picked in his farm. Cousin Gina served a big platter of *Torcinelli,* a Christmas specialty she made just for us. Later, Fernando came in the dining room with his white uniform and a big chef's hat. He greeted everyone and gave us a small glass of *Ciciarilli,* a reddish liqueur his mother, Rosaria, had made with local wild strawberries. We ate and drank all we wanted!

From the dining room, we could see mountains, hills, vineyards, olive trees, and a few sheep grazing. Mamma Lucia wanted me to point out to everyone my grandparents' old farm house.

I asked Luigi and Susan to come outside. I picked a few fig leaves and instructed how to use them. When they returned to the dining room with the leaves in the appropriate places, just like Adam and Eve, the room exploded with laughter. Lorenzo increased the volume of his music and played the *Trenino* (little train) dance. Everybody, even Mamma Lucia, got up, placed their arms on the shoulders of the person in front, and danced around the room, singing and waving their white napkins.

Manduccio Di Giulio is a good friend of mine in Pianella; he owns a large oil mill with many employees. It happened that, when we were at the Vecchio Silos Restaurant, he was celebrating his 80th birthday in a room next to us; he had about fifty guests. I asked all the ladies in my party to go and sing "Happy Birthday" to him. They did, and each lady gave him a warm hug. Manduccio was extremely surprised, honored and overjoyed. He took all the roses on his tables and gave them to those ladies. Soon, he left his party and spent most of the time dancing with my ladies and having pictures taken with them!

We remained in the Vecchio Silos Restaurant until 11:00 p.m. eating, drinking, and dancing. I believe Chef Fernando never had such a fun-loving group in his family restaurant.

Before we left, I called Fernando, Rosaria, Elisabetta, Lorenzo, and all waiters to our tables. We bid them farewell (in Italian, of course) and gave them a deafening round of applause. Then we hugged Mamma Lucia, Cousin Gabriele, Cousin Gina, and bid farewell to them too. *Grazie, Arrivederci, Ciao!* Mamma Lucia came inside the bus and blew a kiss to everybody. She was crying.

On the way back to Hermitage Hotel, some people kept saying: "Seeing the little towns today, meetings relatives, eating such delicious food, and having so much fun: this is what we love most. Remo, today has been the highlight of the entire tour. Grazie."

Dancing at Vecchio Silos

CHAPTER 13

POMPEII: A LOST AND FOUND CITY!

C'era una volta una citta' che si chiamava Pompeii.
(There was once a city called Pompeii).

In Italy, this is how grandfathers begin to tell their grandchildren the sad story of Pompeii. On this Twelfth Day of our tour, my thirty-five enthusiastic "children" not only were told the story of Pompeii, but also walked through the city, touched its ghostly walls, and saw the human remains.

To go to Pompeii, we had to travel from the Adriatic to the Tyrrhenian Sea. That meant a drive from the East to the West Coast, over scenic hills and mountains. That morning, after a good buffet breakfast, we said *Arrivederci* to the gentle staff of Hermitage Hotel, sent a kiss to the blue Adriatic Sea, and took the freeway going west, direction Rome. We bypassed the city of Chieti and drove along the foot of the mighty Maiella Mountain. The sky was clear, but the top of the mountain was covered and rainy.

"I think Maiella is crying because we are leaving," Sandra remarked.

I invited Karen, Mario, Luigi, and Ralph to sit in front of the bus, pick up the microphone, and tell the group about their sentimental journey to the town of their family roots. Since they were still very emotional,

127

their spouses told us the encounter with their Italian relatives. Everyone listened attentively and cheered after hearing their stories.

We made a quick stop in Sulmona, known as *Capital of Confetti* (sugared almonds). Then, we took a scenic mountain road and bypassed the town of Pettorano. Karen took a few pictures of the town and blew a goodbye kiss to her relatives. "I left my heart in Pettorano..." she sang.

Our bus kept climbing higher and higher. The view of the valley below was lovely. We passed by the town of Rocca Pia and came up to the Piano Cinque Miglia (Five Mile Plateau), about 4,000 feet high. As we came out of a tunnel, the village of Rivisondoli, on the left side, suddenly appeared like magic. Next, Roccaraso looked like a neat Swiss village with colorful chalets and ski lifts. From there, the road descended to Castel di Sangro. We enjoyed the view of the valleys below us where cows and sheep were grazing. That reminded me to tell the following story.

"A farmer stands by a river bank. He has with him a wolf, a lamb, and a cabbage. He must take them safely across the river, one by one. Which one do you think he should take first?"

"The wolf," Tony said.

"No, because the lamb will eat the cabbage."

"The cabbage," Betty said.

"No. The wolf will eat the lamb."

"The lamb!" Luigi shouted.

"You are right, because the wolf cannot eat the cabbage. What should he take next?"

"The lamb," answered Peter.

"No. The lamb will eat the cabbage, while the farmer goes back to get the wolf." No one could give the right solution. I explained, "First, the farmer should carry the lamb across the river, then, he should carry the cabbage and take the lamb back. Next, he should take the wolf, and finally go back for the lamb. Problem solved!"

The Italian sky is almost always clear and blue, but with sunshine there must be some rain sometime. Rain poured out of the clouds for about ten minutes as we entered the *Molise* region. However, sunshine greeted us when we arrived at *Campania* region. For many centuries, Campania, and all land south of it, including Sicily, constituted the *Kingdom of Naples*. In 1860, that kingdom conquered by the army lead by Giuseppe Garibaldi, was united to the rest of Italy.

After a short drive into the *Autosdrada del Sole* (Sunshine Freeway), we stopped for lunch at an Autogrill by the city of Caserta. Then, we continued south and soon entered the outskirts of *Napoli* (Naples), Italy's third largest city with more than a million people.

Immediately, Mario sang, "In Napoli, where love is king. When the moon hits your eyes like a big pizza pie, that's amore."

True, Napoli is known as the city of beauty and a*more*. Yet, the city itself does not appeal to tourists; most of them bypass it and go straight to Capri, Amalfi, or Pompeii.

We drove through the outskirts of east Naples, along the base of a mountain with long slopes covered in a green forest. However, that pretty mountain had a huge, reddish, and frightening crater on top. That is the 4200 feet high *Mt. Vesuvius*. It stands as a shocking reminder of the world's most horrific volcanic disaster that buried the entire city of Pompeii some 2000 years ago. Originally, the top of the mountain was pointed like an ice cream cone, but the eruption blew up its top and today a huge valley can be seen in its place.

The freeway sign *Uscita Scavi* (Exit Excavations) meant we had reached our destination. At *Piazza Porta Marina* we found a few restaurants, souvenir shops, and a crowd of tourists. Our guide Alfonso was waiting for us. He introduced himself and kindly greeted everyone. For the next two hours, he walked us through the major streets of old Pompeii, made many stops and explained everything.

"In looking at the gentle slopes around Mt. Vesuvius," said Alfonso, "we realize that, throughout the ages, there have been many eruptions with rivers of lava flowing down. However, Mt. Vesuvius has never acted as badly as it did on August 24 of the year 79 A.D. It woke up with a terrible roar, blew up its entire top and erupted with a savage violence. As the eruption began, a cloud in the shape of a pine tree rose from Vesuvius and soared twenty miles high into the sky. Flames, a hail of pumice stones, volcanic lava, molten ash, hot stones, red scoriae, and sulfuric gas followed the cloud and rained down on Pompeii for three days."

"In the confusion and horror, the unfortunate people of Pompeii tried to escape, but hot ashes, pumice, and sulfuric fumes suffocated and buried them alive. A layer of thirty feet high volcanic matter covered them and their city. Then, there was complete silence and Pompeii, a bustling city of 25,000 people and a favorite holiday destination for the rich Romans, suddenly vanished, remained buried and forgotten for about 1800 years. With time, grass and trees grew on top of the rich volcanic soil and farmers, unaware of what was beneath, cultivated fields, and built houses on top of it."

"However, Pompeii was buried but not destroyed. In 1718, while digging for an underground channel, some workers ran into ancient walls with paintings and inscriptions. Systematic excavations began. Today, one quarter of that city still must be brought back to light. Awakening after a very long sleep, Pompeii is coming back to life and provides an invaluable archeological insight into the ancient Roman life."

"We know that some 2000 years ago mankind reached a remarkable level of civilization in Rome and in other parts of its empire. Then, with the advent of the Barbarians and with centuries of neglect, everything was slowly destroyed. By looking at the Roman ruins today, we can only imagine what Rome was like in ancient times. In Pompeii, on the contrary, we don't have to imagine, because we can see and touch whatever was in that city on the day it was buried. We can look at the very same places where people lived, ate, worked, worshiped, governed, had pleasure, and died. Yes, today Pompeii is like an open window with a full view of its daily life. It is a fascinating educational lesson."

Our guide showed us the *Small Amphitheater* and its gladiators' school; everything in there can be seen just as it was 2,000 years ago. Alfonso sang a Neapolitan song and we could hear him clearly from every corner of the amphitheater; the acoustic system was still perfect. Next, he took us to the *Main Amphitheater* used mostly for gladiator and wild beast shows and combat. We saw the entrance gates, the stone seats and many statues perfectly preserved.

We proceeded through *Via Dell'Abbondanza*, which was Pompeii's main street, full of shops, private houses, and restaurants. The street, wide and straight, is paved with the original large slabs of lava. It had a slightly elevated pedestrian walkway on both sides. Here and there, *stepping stones* facilitated crossing the road without getting the feet wet or dirty. The stepping stones were laid in a way that carts could go through. The visitor can still see the deep *ruts* marked by the chariots' wheels. A few fountains were along the main street. Pompeii's people went there to fetch water for their house needs. However, public buildings and several private villas had their own indoor plumbing. In fact, some lead pipelines that carried water to those places are still visible along the streets and in some villas. There were gutters on the houses and drains on the streets just like the ones we use today.

Our guide, Alfonso, asked us to pause for a moment and, using our imagination, to visualize the chariots driving on the street and hear the rattling of the wheels against the stepping stones. Yes, Via dell'Abbondanza has many stories to tell about its glorious days and the desperation of its terrified people during the eruption.

All buildings in Pompeii were made of volcanic rocks or bricks; they are of a dark red color. The roof of the buildings collapsed under the weight of the volcanic material, but the walls and a few columns are still standing in their original position. Many shops still show grooves for sliding doors in the front. Fast-food shops provided quick service, like our modern restaurants.

Our guide took us inside some inside a couple of ruined villas still decorated with wonderful frescoes, statues, marble tables and mosaic tiles on the floor. The walls had paintings depicting trees, flowers, birds, animals, horseraces, and hunting scenes. Alfonso showed us a bakery with carbonized loaves of bread still in the oven; the oven looks just like a modern pizza oven. There was a wheat grinder and four millstones still in place. A storage room had wine and olive jars and large vats for wine; eggs and fish were waiting to be eaten. There were small bars that used to serve cold and hot beverages.

At a certain point, Mary and Susan could not refrain from laughing.

Alfonso expected that, but kept quiet. Then, he asked, "Ladies, what is so funny?"

"You know what. Well, didn't you see it?" Susan said.

"No, I didn't. What is it?"

"Over there! That thing!"

"What thing?'

Susan blushed, took Alfonso by the hand and showed him a big penis carved into a street stone.

"Oh, yes, that is the phallic symbol etched in the street indicating the direction to a *brothel*. In fact, that is our next stop."

"Is it a casino or a casino' with an accent on the 'O?" Mario wanted to know.

"Oh, boy! I want to see that!" Ralph added.

Around the corner, we found people standing in line to see the *Lupanar*, the oldest known brothel in the world. As a business trade city, many men from out of town visited Pompeii and it served them with some twenty-five brothels. At the entrance door of the Lupanar we saw a big, reddish fresco representing a man displaying his enormous male limb.

"Holy moly! Have you ever seen anything like that?" Bruno exclaimed.

Inside the brothel, we found a big statue of the *God of Fertility* and tiny rooms with a brick platform; the walls had erotic graffiti. One room had this graffiti: "Hic ego puellas multas futui". That is Latin and means, "Here I f— many girls." Tourists came out of there laughing and making funny comments.

Next, we entered the public *baths*, perfectly preserved by its thick roof that withstood the weight of the ashes. Inside the baths, we saw stucco decorations, a changing room with seats, lockers, racks for clothing, a cold room, and a tepid room heated by a large bronze brazier.

Everybody held the breath when we stopped in front of a large storage room containing remains of humans and animals frozen in the position in which they fell when gasses and lava engulfed the city. A young woman lays face down with the head resting on her right arm. A group of twelve people was found in a house. On the threshold of another house, a woman and her three maids lay dead, her jewelry and money scattered around. A group of men, women, and children died while hiding themselves in a tomb. Sixty gladiators were found dead in a gladiators' school. A mule-driver crouched by a wall, covering his face with a cloak against the suffocating whirling ashes. Some people lay on their back and others on their sides. We saw bodies of men, women, and children holding each other in the embrace of death. There was the body of a man with a key in his hand, the body of a slave carrying a wheel barrel and the contorted body of a dog still chained to the door.

Details of those remains were eerily impressive; it really hit us. In most cases those are not real bodies, but *casts* formed by pouring liquid plaster into the cavities left by the decayed bodies of those unfortunate people and animals.

Alfonso walked us to the main square called *forum*. That was the city center containing the courthouse, the temple of Apollo, the temple of Jupiter and a market for wool, meat, and fish. It was also the place where people gathered to buy and sell various other products. Our guide gave a thorough explanation of everything in Pompeii. Finally, through a short cut, he walked us back to Piazza Porta Marina.

Alfonso was an excellent guide; he made the ruins come alive. At a certain point, he asked us to touch a brick wall and think of the man who laid it some 2,000 years ago. What was his personal life like, and how did he feel when Pompeii was buried?

Seeing all the collapsed buildings and people buried under them was a somber and horrifying experience. But, discovering the high-level of culture and civilization reached 2,000 years ago was certainly worth a visit to Pompeii. A two-hour walk through those ruins teaches more than sitting on a school bench for a year.

Pompeii and Mt. Vesuvius

When we went back to the bus, I asked, "What do you think about Pompeii?"

"I feel sorry for all the people who perished there. Couldn't they foresee the disaster?" Joe commented.

"What impressed me most is the fact that, two thousand years ago, people lived in a city that was so close to our modern cities," Mike said.

"I was shocked they had so many brothels. Evidently, the morality was not great. I wonder if the eruption wasn't a repetition of Sodoma and Gomorrah," Sandra lamented.

During the short ride to our hotel, we gave a last look at Mt. Vesuvius and scolded it for what it had done to Pompeii. However, in our hearts we forgave it because, by preserving intact that ancient city, mankind has an opportunity to understand how our forefathers lived some 2,000 years ago.

When we reached the beautiful *Hotel dei Congressi* in Castellammare di Stabbia, the manager, Ernesto, graciously greeted us. He had a "Welcome Brunch" ready for us. That evening our hotel was also host to a large group of vacationers from Germany. They kept me very busy dancing: any time I thought I couldn't dance any more from being out of breath, another lady asked me to dance. We had fun, fun, fun!

CHAPTER 14

THE MAGIC ISLE OF CAPRI

"It was on the Isle of Capri that I found her,
beneath the shade of an old walnut tree."

So goes the song, and on Day Thirteen of our tour, we would experience just that. Yes, we were going to Capri to look for *love*. Perhaps not romantic love for any particular person, but love for nature that Capri inspires to all of its visitors.

As Captain Mariano drove along the lower slopes of Mt. Vesuvius, Peter remarked, "That is insane. Look, people have built their houses even closer to the volcano than the ancient Pompeii. Eventually, it will erupt again and then what? Mariano, hurry, let's get out of here!" Peter was concerned about becoming victim of another volcanic eruption.

We drove to the Port of Naples. For many Italian-Americans that place is a sacred piece of land. It has been referred to as *The Port of Tears*, because in there some hundred years ago many young people embraced for the last time their loved ones, and then embarked for America.

At the Port, we bought tickets for the boat to Capri. While waiting on the dock, an old man, walking among the crowd with a small cart, kept on shouting: "Nocciolini, aranciata, panini, noci di cocco…" (hazelnuts, orange juice, sandwiches, coconuts).

I bought a few nocciolini and shared them with people around me. A young, Asian woman sold roses.

Waiting for the boat, Bruno asked me an interesting question. "Remo, some people told me I am an 'FBI' and my wife is an 'IBM'. Funny, what does it mean?"

"Yes, Bruno, you are a '<u>F</u>ull <u>B</u>lood <u>I</u>talian' and she is an '<u>I</u>talian by <u>M</u>arriage'!"

At 9:00 a.m., a large *hydrofoil boat* pulled up to the dock and the crowd boarded. Soon we crossed the Bay of Naples. The sun was bright and the blue water shining. In the background, we could see the city of Naples and Mt. Vesuvius becoming smaller and the fabled Isle of Capri, ahead of us, getting bigger and bigger, like a mirage.

My enthusiast vacationers sat on the upper deck of the boat. I noticed most women had a rose in their hair. When I enquired why, Betty sang:

"If you go to beautiful Capri, be sure to wear some flower in your hair…"

Next, the duet John and Paul started: "Che aria fresca, pare gia' na festa…. O Sole mio…!" It seemed the opera tenors Luciano Pavarotti and Placido Domingo serenaded us. Paul insisted in Capri he would stand "beneath the shade of an old walnut tree" and wait for love. I am not sure he found the kind of love he was hoping for, but I am certain in Capri everybody fell in love with Mother Nature. People don't go there to admire man-made works of art. They go to admire the beauty of the nature, in particular, the turquoise sea, the blue sky, green hills, mountains, and the perfect weather. In Capri, the combination of all that natural beauty gives the sensation of being in a heavenly place. In fact, when the inhabitants of Capri die and go to heaven, they look around, and say, "Well, nothing new, it looks just like home!"

Yes, Capri is the synonym of beauty, enchantment, fascination, and love. The mild climate, the marvelous coastline, the rocky cliffs, the charming villas, the olive trees, the narrow windings roads, the stunning views of the sea, and the magical beauty make of that island one of the loveliest resorts in the world. It has been an inspiration to painters, artists, poets, writers, lovers, musicians, movie stars, honeymooners, and travelers from around the world. It has been immortalized in books, films, and songs. The Roman Emperors, Tiberius and Augustus, chose to rule the empire from that island.

The Isle of Capri is only about four-mile-long and one and half mile wide. It has two towns, *Capri* (same name as the Island) and *Anacapri*, on a higher plateau. The two towns are linked by a road winding up the cliffs. The town of Capri is the main town and has a population of about 7,000 inhabitants.

Emotions were high when the ferry boat entered *Marina Grande* at 9:45 a.m. and docked at number ten. I bought the tickets for the *Funicolare* (incline cable railway) and we started the ascent to downtown Capri (it is *uptown*!).

Slowly climbing among the tropical vegetation and white houses, the Funicolare reached the top. There we stood on a fashionable terrace, called *La Piazzetta*. It is the heart of the town and the meeting place for locals, holidaymakers, and famous visitors. There are many outdoor cafés where tourists enjoy a drink, listen to Neapolitan music, and watch the rest of the world go by. It has been nicknamed *Il Salotto del Mondo* (The World's Living Room).

What a spectacular view from up there! We felt like being suspended between the blue deep sea and the heavenly blue sky. Some people said they felt like they were in Wonderland. Below us, we saw many white flat-roofed houses, winding streets, orange, fig, and lemon trees with huge lemons. We could see flashy red and yellow convertible cabriolet taxis; they resembled the cars driven by Mr. Rourke and Tattoo on their *Fantasy Island*. The ladies in the cabs looked like divas: they wore silk headscarf and sunglasses. Those fashion-conscious women smiled and waved at everybody.

A young man played the accordion on a corner of La Piazzetta; he had a tip-bucket for people to drop coins into.

Ann grabbed John's hand, and said, "Come on!"

They danced and soon a crowd of admirers gathered around them. Before long, the attention switched to a wedding procession going to the nearby Santo Stefano Church. Next, walking among outside cafés, and then passing under a wide arch by Bar Tiberio, we descended Via Vittorio Emanuele, lined with glamorous design shops, exclusive boutiques, and luxury hotels.

"This street is a shoppers' heaven. Rich and famous people come to shop here. Jacqueline Kennedy loved it," I said.

"Well, if it was good for Jacqueline, it is good for me too!" stated Karen, as she went browsing in a store.

We walked slowly so we could do some window-shopping. Then we passed in front of the famous *Quisisana Hotel,* a super deluxe five-star hotel patronized by a chic and fashionable clientele. We then came to *Via Krupp,* a beautiful, narrow street with lush vegetation, tropical trees, and flowers everywhere. Standing in front of *Profumeria Capri* (a small perfume factory), a lady invited us to sample the fragrance of their products. At a small shop, a few people bought ice cream and a Limoncello drink made with lemons from Capri. We passed by the magnificent architectural complex of the medieval *Carthusian Monastery,* situated among olive trees and vineyards.

A couple of ladies saw the sign *Toilettes* and ran there.

I warned, "Watch out, the old custodian up there likes to pinch women!" While waiting for them, I pointed out the hill with white-dotted villas in the middle of a green pinewood. "Each villa costs millions of dollars. My girlfriend, Sofia Loren, owns one," I said.

"Oh, yes, sure, my girlfriend, Gina Lollobrigida, owns the most expensive one up there!" rebuked Paul.

"Did the old man pinch you?" people wanted to know when the two ladies returned.

"No," he muttered. 'Bella, bella,' (Pretty), and kept on staring at us. We never got close enough for him to pinch."

Next, on the left side of Via Krupp, we climbed a few steps and entered the manicured *Garden of Augustus,* which has a beautiful variety of vegetation, tropical plants and vines of wisteria twining their way up trellises and trees. A few statues adorned the place, among them the statue of Vladimir Lenin was the most remarkable. He visited Capri in 1908.

A few steps further, we found a small iron gate on the left. We climbed a few steps and arrived at a high and steep cliff transformed into a flower decked terrace, called *Belvedere*. The cliff is a small headland that projects right above the deep and crystal turquoise sea. A protective, brick wall ensures no one falls into the precipice some 2,000 feet below.

The panoramic view up there was just spectacular; the sea below was very calm and the sky above was of a deep blue color. Several pleasure boats and luxury yachts floated like toys on the clear water. A few people down there enjoyed sunshine on deck, while others swam. To the left, we could see the majestic and solitary *Faraglioni* rocks rise dramatically from the water like giant fingers toward the sky. Those are three, large rock formations, sculpted over time by the sea and the weather. One Faraglione has a large natural arch through which one can pass in a boat. We could see Marina Piccola and the twisted Krupp Road descending all the way to the beach.

I heard tourists say: "This is unbelievable! This is heaven!"

Luigi got everybody's attention when he sang: "Vedi lu mare quant'e' bello; spira tanto sentimento…" (See how beautiful is the sea; it inspires such a good feeling…). He pretended to be Enrico Caruso.

Yes, we really were in the land of beauty and enchantment, in a natural paradise, on a *Fantasy Island*. It is a perfect place for honeymooners and daydreamers. It is hard to put it into words: some people said it was the prettiest and most breathtaking sight they had ever seen.

While everybody followed me back to the Piazzetta, Paul preferred to remain near the Garden of Augustus. Sipping limoncello on a large glass, he sat on a bench under a huge lemon tree, kept on looking at every woman passing by, and daydreamed.

Back to La Piazzetta, we had one hour of free time to enjoy lunch. At 1:00 p.m., we took the city's yellow mini-bus going up to *Anacapri*, a smaller and quieter town than the town of Capri itself. From remote times and until the year 1870, the only way of reaching Anacapri from the sea was to climb the extremely steep and winding path of 921 steps, called *Strada Fenicia* (Phoenician Road), built by the Phoenicians some 3000 years earlier. Imagine: everything had to be carried up there on back of men and horses!

The current narrow road connecting the town of Capri to Anacapri is a zigzag road literally cut into the side of the mountain. Any time our mini-bus encountered a car or another mini-bus in the opposite direction, it had to slow down, proceed at a crawl, and manage a space of about three inches between the two vehicles. A little mistake and the entire precious load would tumble more than half mile down the cliff. Only expert drivers can operate those mini-buses. Whenever our driver made a scary turn, we closed our eyes and all together screamed for fear and for fun.

Piazza Vittoria is the center of Anacapri. Although there are streets with nice stores and restaurants, tourists love to stroll, shop, and eat in the narrow and quaint footpath called *Via Capodimonte*. At the end of it, one can enjoy a super spectacular view of the sea, of the town of Capri and its port.

In Anacapri, many tourists take the one seat *Seggiovia* (chair lift) and go up to the 3100-foot-high *Mount Solaro*, the island's highest peak. The locals call it "Acchiappanuvole" (clouds catcher). We took the lift and went higher and higher. We dangled our feet over houses, gardens, chestnut and walnut trees, olive groves, vineyards, woods, and bare rock. It is easy to lose a hat or sandals along the way on the lift! It was late September and the vines were loaded with ripe clusters of red and white grapes. Here and there we could see farmers harvesting the grapes. From our chairs, we greeted them and they responded by waving with grapes in their hands. It was a fantastic ride.

At the summit of Mt. Solaro, we found a small snack bar, a panoramic terrace, and a statue of the Emperor Augustus. From up there, we enjoyed a gorgeous panoramic view of the blue sea, brilliant white houses, villas, vineyards, and olive orchards in the green countryside. The sun above us was shining. A gentle breeze caressed our faces and made the women's hair sway. Many seagulls flew close, perhaps to greet us or to look for food. From up there, the whole island seemed to be floating on a blue velvet cloth. The Bay of Naples, Mt. Vesuvius and the Amalfi Coast were clearly visible on the far horizon. We felt as if we had reached the top of the world and could touch the sky. What a spectacular and unforgettable experience!

Tony sang, "Volare, cantare; nel blue dipinto di blue…"

A few men said they were overcome by some mysterious feeling of peace and happiness. Some women insisted they thought they were at the thresholds of heaven. Paul claimed he felt like Moses on Mt. Sinai! I loved Luigi's comment:

"And on the seventh day, God created the Isle of Capri!"

Oh, yes, the top of Mt. Solaro is a perfect place to daydream! However, we also noticed a problem in that terrestrial paradise. The smallest ice cream cone was three Euros at Marina Grande; we paid four Euros at La Piazzetta, five in Anacapri and six on top of Mt. Solaro! Yet, everyone agreed that an ice-cream eaten on Mt. Solaro, between the sea and the heavens, tasted much better than an ice-cream eaten anywhere else.

While descending on my chair lift, I heard someone screaming. Then I saw an Italian woman in her fifties coming up on the chair in the other direction. She was screaming hysterically, kicking her legs and squirming like massive fish caught in a net. She was yelling: "Fatemi scendere, fatemi scendere!" (take me down). Obviously, there was no way she could be taken down before she reached the top of the lift.

When she passed by me, I yelled at her, "Oh, hush up, you big baby!"

She looked at me, and said in amazement, "Cosa hai detto?" (What did you say?) Immediately, she calmed down and became completely silent.

When we returned to Marina Grande, I found Paul still sitting beneath that huge lemon tree. He had been waiting for us. I asked if he had found love. With an ecstatic smile, he responded:

"Oh, yes, I did. Imagine: a beautiful woman walked by, smiled at me and said 'Bonjour, Monsieur. Comment allez-vous? Are you lonesome just like me?' She sat down with me and after a while she invited me to accompany her to the romantic Blue Grotto. I took her there; she kissed me passionately and, when she left she told me, 'Make sure you come to see me in Bordeaux, France.' Oh, what a fantastic day! Remo, could I stay in Capri for the rest of the tour?"

I believe Paul had a daydream.

We concluded our visit to Capri with a feeling of happiness and sadness. We were delighted to see it and sorry we had to leave. We would have loved to stay there a few more days, but, that being impossible, we felt lucky to have seen one of the most beautiful corners of Earth. That evening after dinner, we spent some romantic time on the "Roof Garden" of our hotel. We played a soft music and many people danced under the stars.

Capri: a fantasy island

CHAPTER 15

IN THE FOOTSTEPS OF THE ROMAN CAESARS

On Day Fourteen of our tour, we had a late breakfast. At 9:30, we took freeway A1 going to ROMA (Rome), *Caput Mundi* (Capital of the World)), *The Eternal City* and *Cradle of Western Civilization*. The enthusiasm among my people was very high. I heard them say:

"Today, my name is Julius Caesar!"

"And I am Cleopatra!"

"I am Spartacus, the gladiator!"

"Watch out, I am Brutus!"

After we passed by the city of Frosinone I gave this brief historic account about the origins of Rome. "When the Greeks destroyed the city of Troy, more than 3000 years ago, Prince Aeneas and several soldiers escaped and traveled across the Mediterranean Sea, searching for a suitable place to rebuild their city. Carthage and Sicily seemed good places, but the gods pushed them to *Latium* (today's Lazio, where Rome is located). A population of shepherds, the *Latins*, lived there. Their king, Latinus, welcomed Aeneas and gave him his daughter Lavinia in marriage. Soon, Aeneas became king and for the next 700 years the first male born was king of the Latins. After many years, Prince Amulius decided to break away from the tradition. He secretly kidnapped his older brother, Numitor, and proclaimed himself king. To

144

eliminate any threat to his throne, he forced his niece, Princess Rhea Silvia, to become a priestess. Under penalty of being buried alive, a priestess could not marry."

"From up above, the god Mars went to visit Rhea Silvia and nine months later two twin brothers were born; those are the famous Romulus and Remus, founders of Rome. Very angry, bad King Amulius ordered the mother and her children to be killed. However, the babies were secretly placed in a basket and abandoned along the Tiber River, just like Moses. A merciful she-wolf found and fed them. Miracle or myth? Shepherd Faustulus rescued the twins and raised them. Later, when they were told the truth, they killed Amulius, found their grandfather Numitor and restored him to the throne. As a reward, Romulus and Remus were given ownership and full authority over the little piece of land where they grew up. There they built a village, declared it *free city* and welcomed anybody to settle within. Soon, that tiny village became filled with outlaws, bandits, and outcasts. Those were the first Romans! After Remus' death, Romulus named that village *Roma* (Rome) in honor of his brother. It was the year 753 BC."

"Rome's first inhabitants were all men; they needed women if their tiny nation had to survive; but the neighboring women refused to marry those bandits. Through deceit, many women were kidnapped and a cruel war ensued. The first Romans were hardened criminals, therefore, they won the war and the neighboring towns were annexed to Rome. Over the years and through many wars, the little nation expanded and annexed all the local tribes: the Sabines, Etruscans, Samnites, Marsi, Volsci, Equi, Tarantini, Piceni, Peligni, Apuli, and Marruccini. By the year 300 B.C., the Romans had full control of the Italian peninsula. After the Carthaginian wars in 146 B.C., most of North Africa and Spain came under Roman rule. Julius Caesar brought Western Europe and England under the power of Rome. Eventually, at about 300 years A.D. most of the world known was living under Roman laws."

"We know that later the *Barbarians* came from central Europe and destroyed the mighty Roman Empire. While at the peak of its old glory

Rome was a city of more than a million people, but after its inglorious fall it became a rural town of about 15,000 inhabitants. The entire city of Rome became a ghost town. Consequently, all buildings deteriorated, collapsed and the ground level went up. Soon, grass and trees grew over the rubble and the glory that was Rome laid buried some forty feet down below. Actually, the luxurious palaces we admire today are all built on the ashes of the defunct Rome of the Caesars."

I lectured for about twenty minutes and when I finished most people applauded.

However, Marc, sitting close to me, was sleeping! He suddenly woke up, and said, "What, what? Are we in Rome?"

Not quite there; we had just reached the *Raccordo Anulare* (bypass), and we were thus at the threshold of the Eternal City.

Today, Rome has expanded considerably and its population has increased to more than four million. Basically, the city we see now consists of three distinct parts: The *New Rome* (outside the Aurelian Walls), the *Rome of the Renaissance* (inside the Aurelian Walls) and the *Rome of the Caesars* (dead and buried under Rome of the Renaissance). Visitors are primarily interested in the Rome of the Caesars', but only a small portion of it has been excavated and that is mostly in the area around the Coliseum and the Forum.

To enter Rome, most victorious Roman generals and their armies traveled with coaches and chariots through the bumpy Appian Way. My small army of thirty-five tourists traveled on a comfortable bus along a modern freeway and entered the Eternal City through *Via Porta Latina*.

A real spirit of excitement and suspense overwhelmed everybody as we entered the historic Rome. Soon, on our left side we saw ghostly remains of cyclopean brick walls and huge arches of a reddish color. The grandeur of *Rome of the Caesars* unveiled.

"By Hercules, what is that?" John wondered.

"Those are the colossal ruins of the *Baths of the Emperor Caracalla*," I explained. "They were built in 212 A.D. The building complex is immense; a real town. Imagine: it took five years to level the ground and prepare the hydraulic and drainage system before building began. Those baths were fifty feet high, consisted of several floors and could accommodate 2000 bathers at one time. Inside were Olympic-size pools for cold, warm, and hot baths. The largest pool was one hundred eighty feet long. There were steam rooms, massage rooms, sauna, gymnasiums, wrestling, boxing rooms and swimming pools. The leisure facilities consisted of recital halls, libraries, art galleries, barber shops, hairdressers, restaurants, and even brothels."

"The interior of the baths was completely covered with marble and statues depicting athletes and acrobats. There were alleys lined with sculptures and fountains. The statue of Asclepius measured fifteen feet high. The floors contained symmetrical black and white patterns made of mosaic. The main entrance door had an inscription: *'Mens sana in corpore sano'* (A healthy mind in a healthy body). The ancient Romans valued their physical health so much that they defined an ignorant man as 'Someone who does not know how to read or swim.' Yes, those baths were a true masterpiece of architecture and hydraulic engineering."

We stopped in front of those baths, but did not go inside. I asked people to use their imagination and let the ruins tell them what the baths were like some 2000 years ago. It seemed we could see coaches, like our taxis, dropping off and picking up people. We could almost hear the water splashing and see carefree men coming out with a towel on their shoulder and conversing in a strange language.

Unfortunately, with the advent of the Barbarians in the 5th century, those luxurious facilities were abandoned, reduced to ruins and later became veritable quarries for marble and other building materials. The ruined walls and the empty arches we see today look like desolate dwellings of dead giants. Yet, those ruins still offer an excellent insight into the social life of the ancient Romans.

Just a little further down we encountered the famous *Circus Maximus,* which was built about 2000 years ago in a natural hollow between the Aventine and Palatine Hills. It measured 2037 feet in length and

387 feet in width. All around it there were three superimposed arcades with seats that accommodated at least 150,000 spectators.

The circus was used for athletic tournaments, parades, public feasts, religious and military ceremonies, public executions, gladiator shows, beast hunt, and long-distance foot races, but its main function was to hold *chariot and horse races.* Charioteers had to compete in races with chariots usually pulled by four, six or eight mettlesome horses. Besides competing in races, the athletes had to stand on running horses, jump from one horse to the other, from one chariot to the other and pick up a cloth from the ground at full gallop.

We can imagine the circus packed with thousands of people cheering as the horses' hooves thundered. We can almost see the rumbling chariots and hear the noise, the cheers, and the excitement of the exhilarated crowd. It must have been astounding. Romans had a passionate love for horseracing. One should watch a movie such as *Julius Caesar, Ben Hur, The Gladiator* to get an insight into the splendor and excitement that once was the Circus Maximus. The emperor observed the games from his palace on the Palatine Hill.

Unfortunately, that glorious place also was later abandoned. Its marble and other materials were removed and used to build Renaissance palaces. Today, the original lower level of the circus lays buried under some twenty feet of alluvial soil and accumulated debris. Today, there isn't too much to see except for the elongated oval outline of what was once a huge racetrack. We can still see the basis of its ruined *Spina* in the middle and a tower sticking out of the ground on the south end. The Circus Maximus is just a grass land used for walking, jogging, playing *bocce* (lawn bowling), picnicking, practicing *soccer*, hosting huge crowds at music concerts, and rallies.

We drove all around Circus Maximus and stopped at Piazzale Romolo; we took pictures. Then I asked, "Have you ever seen Caesar's Palace?"

"Yes, in Las Vegas!" replied Ralph.

"Well, look up on that Palatine Hill, straight in front of you. Do you see that massive red brick palace? It is the real Caesar's Palace!"

Rome: Caesar's Palace with Circus Maximus on foreground

Everyone remained astounded. What an historic place! The Palatine is the Hill on which Rome was born in the year 753 B.C.; it is the cradle of the Imperial Rome. Through the centuries, the Hill was embellished with luxurious palaces entirely covered with the most beautiful marble. Imagine: the cruel Emperor Domitianus, afraid of being stabbed in the back, had all marble floors waxed every day. This allowed him to see reflections, like in a mirror, if anyone was near! Yet, despite his efforts, he was murdered. Julius Caesar, Augustus, Tiberius, Vespasian, Titus, Marcus Aurelius, Claudius, Trajanus, Diocletianus, Antoninus, Hadrianus, and many other emperors lived in that royal palace. Think: while most of the world was living in huts, the Romans were living in palaces covered with gold and precious marble!

Mario insisted he saw the ghost of Marc Anthony and Cleopatra kissing on a balcony. Angelo said he spotted the Emperor Caligula on the top terrace, gesticulating and waving frantically. Caligula had betted on his favorite horse running in the Circus Maximus. Obviously, Mario and Angelo had a vivid imagination.

Alas, during the Dark Ages, the flamboyant and ornate emperors' palace was also abandoned and later became a free quarry for hunters of artistic items and building material. Today, a visitor can see only numerous cyclonic red brick walls, empty arches, and bare foundations.

149

The entire complex looks like a dilapidated dwelling of enormous giants. Yet, the few remaining ruins are still impressive and show the former grandeur of Imperial Rome.

Luigi shouted, "Dear Caesars, we feel sorry for what time and looters have done to your house! Too bad home insurance was not available in olden times!"

On San Gregorio Street, we passed under an ancient and broken *Aqueduct* which carried water to Caesar's Palace. Yes, Imperial Rome had fourteen aqueducts supplying water to eleven public baths and 1350 fountains throughout the city.

Finally, Captain Mariano dropped us off right in front of the Coliseum and we began our walking tour through the heart of the ancient Rome. As we sat foot on the ground, we came face-to-face with the famous *Colosseum,* the most thrilling of Rome's ancient sights, the symbol of the power and glory of ancient Rome and one of the world's biggest tourist attractions. What a magnificent creation of the human intelligence! For a moment, people remained speechless and motionless. Suddenly, it seemed we had gone back in time some 2000 years. That view recalled vivid images of the rise and fall of the Roman Empire, the Caesars, the gladiatorial combat, and the Christians devoured by lions. We could almost hear the gladiators shouting, "Hail Caesar!" It seemed that any moment thousands of spectators, dressed in the finest clothes, would stagger out laughing and inebriated.

The Colosseum was built in 80 A.D. by Emperor Vespasian and his son, Titus, with the labor of 100,000 slaves captured in the Jewish war. It was built with travertine material on the outside and tufa and bricks in the interior. The main pedestals were built of marble blocks. Using 200 wagons and 400 oxen every day, the slaves moved the building materials from the quarries some twenty-five miles away. At the same time, thousands of other slaves, professional builders, stonecutters, bricklayers, sculptors, architects, and numerous other laborers worked at the building site.

The façade of the Colosseum is 187 feet high; that means about the height of fifteen modern stories. The earthquake of 847 damaged and brought down part of the top floor, as we can see today. The ground floor has seventy-six entrance arches, each still numbered with Roman numerals. Those entrances were for the public. Four other entrance arches were for the emperor, magistrates, wealthy patricians, senators, and Vestal Virgins. The numerous archways ensured that, in an emergency, the Colosseum could be emptied within minutes. The seats were made of marble. The second and third floors were also constructed with arches and at that time had 160 statues of deities and other figures from mythology. Around the perimeter of the inside arena was a wall high enough to prevent the wild beasts from leaping up into the lower range of seats. When completed, the Colosseum was entirely sheathed with marble and could accommodate 50,000 spectators.

The Romans went to the Colosseum to watch the *Ludi* (games). The games were held to commemorate the emperors' birthday, a military victory, an election triumph, funerals, executions, or other special occasions. Among the most popular *games* was the combat between gladiators. Some gladiators were blindfolded on horseback and fighting other gladiators; they fought also against lions and tigers; often there were fights between horsemen and animal hunts. At times, the Colosseum was flooded for mock naval combat re-playing famous Roman victories.

The show in the Colosseum usually began with a flamboyant parade featuring Roman officials, musicians, dancers, priests, and images of gods. The emperor and his entourage followed; then started the carnage of wild animals hunted down in the arena. The gladiators fight to death was next and exhilarated the crowd. Yes, the Romans had an insatiable lust for bloody games. To see men being killed that way was very entertaining for them.

Most gladiators were prisoners of war, slaves, criminals, or men indebted. They had the choice to fight and regain their freedom or to remain prisoners or slaves.

Before starting the fight, they had to greet the emperor: "Ave, Caesar. Morituri te salutant!" (Hail Caesar, those who are about to die salute you!) With their thumbs, the spectators decided the defeated gladiator's fate: thumbs up meant he should live; thumbs down meant he should be killed.

How many people died in the Colosseum? Only God knows. Historians report that, during the hundred days of festivities for its inauguration in 80 A.D., at least 9000 wild beasts and some 2000 gladiators lost their lives. To celebrate his victory in Dacia, the Emperor Trajan staged combats involving 11,000 wild beasts, and 10,000 gladiators. During a special festival in 240 A.D. the following were slaughtered: 2000 gladiators, seventy lions, forty wild horses, thirty elephants, thirty leopards, twenty wild asses, nineteen giraffes, ten elks, ten hyenas, ten tigers, and many hippopotamus, crocodiles, oxen, panthers, bears and ostriches. On another occasion, a hundred lions were brought into the arena at the same time; their roar was so deafening the spectators suddenly became speechless and feared for their own lives. Most of those beasts were imported from Africa and Middle East. At least forty-two emperors witnessed that carnage at the Coliseum.

Many ruthless emperors used the Colosseum to murder tens of thousands of Christians by stoning, crucifixion, burning at the stake or feeding them to hungry wild animals. Some Christians were covered with the skin of wild beasts and left to be eaten by dogs. The cruelest Emperor Nero even introduced the *twilight executions:* Christians were nailed to a cross and burned alive as torches to light the Coliseum. Executions of Christians provided a popular midday entertainment!

For about 300 years those hideous crimes amused the decadent Romans. To understand the horror in the Colosseum one should watch movies such as *Quo Vadis, Spartacus,* or *Gladiator.* It was only in the year 312 A.D. that Emperor Constantine prohibited persecutions against the Christians, and in 399 A.D. the Emperor Honorius completely abolished the gladiatorial fights. By then, Rome had become a Christian city.

When the Barbarians ruled in Rome, the Colosseum was abandoned and despoiled of its statues, decorations, and marble; they even removed the bronze clamps holding the stones together and made swords with them. The removal of those clamps left numerous holes in the building, which still scar it today. Then, the Colosseum fell into complete neglect; soon it became overgrown with weeds, trees, flowering plants, and some exotic specimens that grew from seeds brought in by the animals from far-away places. In the Middle Ages, the vaulted spaces in the arches and under the seating of the Coliseum were used as housing, work-shops, and quarters for a religious order and fortress.

At the dawn of the Renaissance, the Colosseum became a free quarry, where people went to get material for new palaces, churches, hospitals, and public buildings. Recently, it has been revered as *sacred* and, where the emperors once sat, now is a Cross in remembrance of the many Christians who died there.

Today, the Colosseum looks as if some hideous monster has eaten most of it. The structure we see standing represents the leftovers of that destruction. Yet, despite its ruined state and its sad history, the Colosseum remains one of the most outstanding symbols of Imperial Rome and one of the most fascinating historic sites in the world.

Rome: the inside of the Colosseum today

I took my group inside the Colosseum; we touched the same walls once soaked with the blood of so many victims. We even stood in the spot where the emperors sat. The emotion of being there was overwhelming, almost frightening. It recalled the helpless cry of the innocent Christians, the roar of the hungry lions, the clash of the gladiators' swords and the yelling of the crowd thirsty for blood.

It was about 1:00 p.m. when we came out of the Colosseum. I gave an hour and a half of free time for lunch and browsing around. I advised: "If you want to eat lunch, go to the street behind the Colosseum. There you will find plenty of good restaurants and pizza places. I recommend you buy a book that shows Rome as it was then and as it is today. Be back to this same spot at 2:30. Now go, my Romans, go!"

In the meantime, when I saw several tourists sitting and eating lunch on a few broken columns lying by the Colosseum, I bought a *panino* (sandwich) and joined them. A swarm of hungry pigeons came around us.

An elderly woman from my group preferred to stay with me, and later asked, "Are these pigeons male or female?"

How could I know? Even if I had them in my hands I could not tell!

At 2:30 p.m., my thirty-five *Romans* regrouped by the Arch of Constantine. Right after I took the roll call, Peter asked:

"Remo, what is this colossal monument here?"

Before I could answer, Marc replied: "This is the *Arch of Constantine*, the emperor who won a civil war against Maxentius in 312 A.D. He granted freedom of religion."

"Bravo!" I complimented Peter.

Next, we walked along the elegant *Via dei Fori Imperiali*, which is a wide elevated street running among the ancient ruins from the Colosseum to Piazza Venezia. The street was made by Benito Mussolini in 1932 to revive the former glory of the Roman Empire. At the beginning of Via dei Fori Imperiali, visitors can admire four huge marble and bronze *maps* posted by Mussolini to show the expansion of the Roman Empire. The maps show that from a tiny little village the Eternal City grew to an immense country. In fact, for more than a thousand years the might of Rome united millions of people under one law, one religion, one language, one civilization, and one world from Spain to Arabia and from England to Egypt.

Walking along said Via dei Fori Imperiali is like walking into history: one comes in direct contact with what was once the bustling and pulsating heart of the political, commercial, and religious activity of ancient Rome, known as *Roman Forum*. For hundreds of years that area was adorned with extravagant temples, palaces, government offices, courts of law, markets, shops, monuments, honorary columns, memorials, fountains, triumphal arches, shops, and statues. Emperor Augustus used to say:

"I found Rome a city of brick and left it a city of marble."

At that time, every day a multitude of people poured into the Forum to conduct commercial affairs, banking, shopping, and marketing. They came to watch festivals, religious ceremonies, triumphal military processions, political speeches, elections, criminal trials, or simply to meet their friends. To see the full splendor of the Forum Romanum, we should have been there the latest 1700 years ago.

Alas! Around the year 300 A.D., the glorious Roman Empire showed signs of weakness. Political and military corruption, decline of morals, earthquakes, plagues, and inept and inhuman emperors contributed to the disintegration of Rome. Imagine: in a hundred years, there were thirty-seven emperors and of those twenty-two were murdered for incompetence and cruelty. The Barbarians brought the final blow to the Roman civilization. The city of Rome was invaded, plundered, and burned by the Visigoths. More hordes of Barbarians followed: the Vandals, Ostrogoths and Longobards; they brought nothing but destruction and misery. In 476 A.D., the Roman Empire crumbled and came to an end.

With the advent of the Barbarians, the city of Rome fell into disarray and its marvelous Forum was abandoned. Gradually, the population decreased and, from a city of over a million inhabitants, Rome became a ghost town of only 15,000. Consequently, with time, the buildings in the Forum collapsed and later plunders stripped them of statues, marble, tumbled stones, and building materials. Only unusable materials were left in place. The great Forum Romanum became a dumping ground, and then some forty feet of debris and sediment from the surrounding hills covered everything. Wild grass grew on it and cows, goats, and cattle traders settled on top. In fact, in the Middle Ages that entire area became known as *Campo Vaccino* (Cattle Field). It was not until the eighteenth century the Forum began to be excavated. The digging is still ongoing and today it reveals the complete desolate state of what once was the glorious Rome. Let us take a walk through it.

First, we looked at Forum Romanum from the elevated Via dei Fori Imperiali. What did we see? It is hard to describe it. A realistic analogy is that down there we saw a huge *cemetery* with open graves showing bits and pieces of broken skeletons and fractured bones. It was the cemetery of the Imperial Rome!

Then, we descended into that cemetery, walked among those skeletons, and got a closer look at that ghostly place. Again, what did we see? We saw whatever had been discarded and left over by the looters. Specifically, we discovered an utterly chaotic pile of rubbles, fragments of sumptuous temples and basilicas, fallen or mutilated walls, bits of marble columns, sections of sculpted marble friezes with beautiful decorations and inscriptions, broken decorative capitols, and cornices. A few granite columns are what remain of the temple of Saturn; only three lone columns from the temple of Castor and Pollux stand up. Here was the floor-plan of a vanished temple; there were cracked and fluted columns lying on the ground. Jumbled blocks of ancient marble covered by dust and weeds lay everywhere. Stumps of brick pillars can be seen under olive trees. The rostra, on top of which great politicians and legislators stood to speak to the crowds, now stand mutilated.

We saw a row of broken columns standing up like lone ghosts. Other scarred columns were supporting a fragmented lintel or architrave. Several dilapidated foundations and smashed floors made us imagine the sumptuous buildings that once were there. A broken sewer revealed that Romans were excellent builders and engineers. Some structures looked like architectural freaks with a 2000-year-old first floor and a modern edifice on top of it. The temple of Antoninus and Faustina has been converted into a Christian church. Its front marble columns, still standing, show the deep grooves made by the barbarians attempting to tear them down. The cords burned into the columns! Of the splendid Basilica Julia only the floor plan remains. The glorious Via Sacra, once Rome's main street adorned with monuments and statues, now shows only bits and pieces of stone pavement with ruts made by chariots. The huge brick buildings on the side of Capital Hill overlooking the Forum, look like open caverns inhabited by giants. Many more ancient constructions have completely disappeared and are now covered by laurel and olive trees.

Tony touched a few statues with missing limbs. Mary walked frantically among the ruins and took pictures of broken architraves, fragments of lintels, broken bases of columns, pieces of staircases, tops of altars, cracked marble pavements, remnants of marble steps, and broken columns. Defying the prohibition, Paul climbed on a low podium stripped of its marble statue and posed as the almighty Jupiter.

Yes, the Forum is the real cemetery of an extinct Roman grandeur. The almighty Rome of the Caesars lies down there, as dead as it could be. *Sic transit gloria mundi!* (Thus, ends the glory of this world).

Upon seeing that cemetery, an eerie feeling overcomes the visitor. Some people sit in the ruins and imagine the splendid buildings that for centuries witnessed the greatest events of Roman history. Nowhere are specters of the past more palpable than in the Forum. To stand in the political, business, and religious center of the Roman Empire brings shivers to one's body. Yes, the language of those ruins is very eloquent: even in decay, they are silent witnesses of the splendor and glory that was Rome. If those stones could talk, each of them would have some marvelous story to tell. *Roma quanta fuit ipsa ruina docet!* (Those same ruins tell how great Rome was).

From an historical perspective, the Forum Romanum is more interesting than the Colosseum in that people went to the Colosseum only to be entertained. But the Romans were not just idlers, seeking only physical pleasure; they were also excellent builders, clever politicians, skilled soldiers, shrewd businessmen and profoundly religious. It was in the Roman Forum that those skills and opinions were first developed, discussed, and adopted. We can say Western Civilization was born in the Roman Forum.

While wandering into that cemetery of the Roman glory, we found a few surprises: the Arches, the Curia, and the Pool of the Vestals. Those constructions have been preserved almost in their entirety. The Arch of Titus commemorates his victory over the Jews and the Arch of Septimius Severus is to celebrate the defeat of the Parthians. Both arches are in marble and among the best preserved ancient Roman monuments, although a little tarnished by time.

In the middle of the Forum, we found a large and well preserved brick building, called *Curia* or *Senate House*. It stands alive and well, like a lone survivor in a huge battlefield. The interior has been stripped of all its marble, but it still has its original walls, roof, three large windows on the back, and one window on each side. The Curia owes its survival to the fact it was turned into the church of St. Adrian. We stood on the same steps of the Curia where Julius Caesar was murdered 44 B.C. and then we visited the nearby small brick altar where his body was cremated. Suddenly, a loud voice was heard: "Et tu, Brute, fili mi!" (You too, Brutus, my son). No, it was not Caesar, but our Luigi decrying that historic assassination.

The *Pools of the Vestals* was used by the six virgin women who had the duty of keeping the Sacred Fire of Viesta, goddess of hearth. The Sacred Fire was symbol of the eternal life of Rome. Under penalty of being buried alive, the Vestals had to observe the vow of chastity for thirty years. In return for their service, they were housed in a two-floor marble palace with fifty rooms and three swimming pools adorned with statues. Unbelievable: the swimming pools are still intact and most statues, although some partially mutilated, are still on their pedestals.

The Barbarians and the plunders did not touch them. Perhaps they believed in Vesta's curse:

"Whoever bathes in the Vestals' waters will die of a violent death!"

Luisa and Betty posed as Vestal Virgins!

As we kept on wandering among the ruins, Marc asked: "What does SPQR stand for? I see it in many places."

"That stands for *The Senate and the Roman people*. It was the Senate's seal on official documents."

Rome: the Forum Romanum today

We visited the gloomy and dreadful subterranean cells called *Mamertine Prison*. That is where some of Rome's most notorious vanquished enemies were imprisoned and left to die of starvation or strangulation. St. Peter and St. Paul too were held there until they were miraculously set free. A legend says St. Peter caused a spring to well up in the prison so he could baptize his fellows prisoners and guards.

On our way back to Via Fori Imepriali, Luisa asked, "Remo, when I was in Rome many years ago, I saw a lot of wild cats sunbathing on top of these ancient pillars and ruins. I see only few now. Why?"

"Luisa, what do you think you ate at the hotel last night?" I answered jokingly.

"No! Tonight, I will not eat at the hotel!" she screamed.

Some people taunted: "Meow! Meow!"

Truthfully, recently the city authorities have declared those cats to be a health hazard.

On both sides of Via dei Fori stand a few large bronze statues of famous Roman emperors. John greeted the statue of *Julius Caesar*:

"Buon Giorno, Caesar!"

Then Bruno said, "Hello, Augustus, would you like a coke?"

Both Caesar and Augustus seemed to look at us, but neither one returned our greeting. I am sure they did not understand Italian or English or maybe they were too much distressed about the pitiful way the barbarians had reduce their beloved Rome.

Next, we stopped by a street mime dressed like the famous Latin writer, *Cicero*. He kept on declaiming: "O tempora o mores!" (Oh, the times! Oh, the customs! Alas, how times and morals have changed for the worse!).

Peter dropped a few coins in the mime's bucket, and told him, "Wake up, man. We are in the twenty-first century!"

Next, on the right side of Via dei Fori, we saw a large semicircular red-brick building with many arches. "That is the *Trajan's Market*, built in 110 A.D.," I explained. "It is considered the first shopping mall in the world. It had marble porticos and one hundred fifty shops. Next to it stands the ninety-foot-tall *Trajan's Column* which contains 2500 bas-reliefs describing his victory over Dacia, the modern Romania. The emperor's ashes were kept in a golden urn at the base of that column."

After spending most of the day in the Roman ruins, we finally returned into the reality of modern life: we were in *Piazza Venezia*. They say that "All roads lead to Rome." Where exactly? They lead to Piazza Venezia, which is the heart of modern Rome. On the south side stands the enormous white marble building called *Altare della Patria* (Altar of the Fatherland), built by Sacconi in 1885. The building was erected in honor of King Emanuele II who united Italy in 1870. The King can be seen riding a colossal bronze horse. The tomb of the *Unknown Soldier* is there too, guarded by two soldiers. Americans have surnamed that gigantic white monument *The Wedding Cake*. In fact, seen from a distance, it looks just like that. Others call it: "The Typewriter" and "The False Teeth".

With the Wedding Cake to our backs, on the left side we caught a glimpse of a large, brownish palace. "That is *Palazzo Venezia*. Mussolini used it as Fascist Headquarters. Through the years of Fascism, he harangued his followers from that tiny balcony jutting out from the front of the palace," I explained.

It was about 5:00 p.m. and our feet began to complain. Mariano picked us up on the left side of said Wedding Cake. We visited more historic sites from the comfort of our bus. We saw *Isola Tiberina* (Island of Tiber) and the *Ponte Rotto* (Broken Bridge), the oldest stone bridge in Rome built 2200 years ago. By the church of Santa Maria in Cosmedin we noticed people standing in line to place their hand inside the mouth of a huge marble mask, called *La Bocca della Verita* (The Mouth of the Truth). They say if you tell lies, a nasty ghost bites your hand. That was an ancient drain cover found in a recent excavation.

"Remo, stop the bus. Joe, go, put your hand in there. I want to see if you really love me," Laura insisted.

"Honey, why do you ask that? I would never cheat on you!" Joe pleaded.

Then, we passed by the temple of *Fortuna Virilis* (Temple of Manly Fortune), which has been preserved intact. I explained old and impotent Roman men went to pray there to regain their manly strength. It is no wonder why the Barbarians did not destroy it: they too needed it!

We drove by the *Teatro Marcello,* an open-air theater used mostly for performance of drama and music. It could easily accommodate 20,000 spectators. Imagine: today, the Romans have built luxurious apartment houses on the upper portion of its ruined walls.

Finally, we passed by the 120 feet tall *Piramide Cestia,* covered with white marble. It was built in 12 B.C. by the wealthy Gaius Cestius as funerary monument for his family. Passing through *Porta San Paolo* (St. Paul Gate), we left ancient Rome. That Gate is part of the twelve-mile-long and fifty-two-foot-high insurmountable *Mura Aureliane* (Aurelian Walls) built to protect Rome against the invading Barbarians. Imagine: the glorious, wealthy, and powerful Rome had to lock itself inside those walls to escape from the Barbarians. Yet, even those walls were unable to prevent the great Roman Empire from being annihilated.

Our day was over. Mamma Mia, what an educational experience! We were exhausted, but overwhelmed by the quantity and significance of the history we had learned. They say Rome was not built in one day, but in many centuries; yet, we discovered it in one day!

Rome: Castle San Angelo

CHAPTER 16

DISCOVERING OUR CHRISTIAN HERITAGE

"Quo vadis, Domine?"
"Eo Romam iterum crucifigi"
(Where are you going, Lord?
I am going to Rome to be crucified again)

Those were the words exchanged between St. Peter and the Lord Jesus on the Appian Way, just outside Rome. Aware of the importance of bringing the Gospel to the heart of the Roman Empire, St. Peter left Jerusalem and went to Rome. There his mission was quite successful, but, facing crucifixion under the Emperor Nero, he abandoned the Christian community and ran for his life. On the Appian Way, he met the Lord, who was going to Rome to continue the work the apostle had abandoned. Jesus knew he would be crucified again in that pagan city. Ashamed of his lack of courage, Peter returned to Rome, continued his mission, and later was crucified there. A little church, called *Quo Vadis,* can be seen where the two met. Inside that church, the footprints on an ancient stone are believed to be those of Jesus.

The first Christians built a little chapel on Peter's tomb and soon it drew pilgrims. Later, the Emperor Constantine replaced that chapel with a magnificent basilica, which stood for more than 1,000 years. By the beginning of the 15th century the structure of that basilica was un-safe: the walls on the central nave were more than three feet off the per-pendicular! Pope Julius II had it torn down and hired the architect Bramante to begin building a new basilica. It was completed in 1615, after 109 years of intense work. Many famous architects and artists worked on it, including Bernini, Michelangelo, Raphael, Rossellino, Pe-ruzzi, Sangallo, Vignola, and Maderno.

The Basilica we admire today is about 400 years old and covers an area of 5.7 acres, measures 730 feet long and 452 feet high; it contains eleven chapels, forty-five altars and more than a hundred tombs for popes, emperors, kings, and queens. A total of 60,000 people can fit inside.

Architecturally, the Basilica is the most stunning achievement of the Renaissance period and one of the greatest creations of the human in-telligence. Artistically, it is a priceless museum for its infinite works of art. It is a lasting testament to civilization and to the glory of God.

Some people have criticized the new Basilica as being too extrava-gant. Well, the Egyptians, the Greeks and the Romans built magnificent temples to their many gods. The Muslims have their elaborate mosques and Buddha has his splendid temples. Doesn't the God of the Christians deserve the best that Christians can offer?

For the past 2,000 years, millions of pilgrims from all over the world have been going to St. Peter's Basilica to profess their faith. Like those pilgrims, the objective for Day Fifteen of our Tour was to visit that Basil-ica and to thank St. Peter and the first Christians for making it possible for us to practice our religion. No, we were not in danger of being cru-cified or devoured by lions.

It was a clear and mild day when we left the hotel and headed for Vatican City. On the way, I gave this short account of that most revered place. "When the Roman Empire fell under the domination of the Bar-barians total chaos reigned in the Eternal City. People found a certain protection only in the Christian Church and, in particular, in the person of the Pope who more and more was considered as their spiritual and political leader. In fact, it was Pope Leo I who in 452, armed only with a cross, stopped Attila, the terrible king of the Huns. It was Pope Gregory who prevented the Ostrogoth King Totila from attacking Rome. It was Pope Gregory II who stopped the invasion of the Longobards and converted to Christianity their King Liutprand. Pope Leo III succeeded in joining several barbarian kingdoms into one single power, called the *Holy Roman Empire*. Besides providing leadership and guidance to the universal church, later the Popes even anointed and crowned emperors and regulated disputes among them. Thus, when Rome ended its political mission, the Christian Church provided leadership and helped restore order, promoted morality, civilized the barbarians and continued the spiritual mission handed down by St. Peter and by the thousands of Christian martyrs."

"In the year 800 A.D., Charlemagne, King of the Franks, gave the Church complete sovereignty over a large piece of land in central Italy, which became known as the *State of the Church*. The State lasted until 1870 when it was taken away by the newly formed Italian Kingdom. However, in 1929 the Italian government granted complete political independence to the very tiny piece of land (only 110 acres) called *Citta' del Vaticano* (Vatican City). Although it is the smallest country in the world, it has enormous religious and historic importance. The border separating it from Italy is just a metal fence along the outer perimeter of St. Peter's Square. There is no passport requirement to enter."

"Today, Vatican City has its own constitution, its ties with the nations around the world, its flag, its national anthem and its coat of arms. It has even its own radio and TV station, train station, post office, stamps, and outstanding museums. That tiny state is the spiritual center for the world's more than one billion Catholics. It is also the heart of Christendom, because St. Peter, whose remains are in Vatican City, is the Vicar of Christ. *Ubi Petrus ibi Ecclesia* (Where is Peter there is the Church). Today, more than ever pilgrims travel from across the globe to pray on St. Peter's tomb to participate in papal liturgies and to attend public audiences."

As we came closer to Vatican City, I noticed a much heavier traffic; tourist busses were dropping off their passengers everywhere. It was Wednesday and thus thousands of people were going to the *Pope's Audience* on St. Peter's Square. It was about 9:30 a.m. when we crossed the *Tiber River* and entered the historic section of Rome.

I said, "Stand by; you are going to have a big surprise."

Captain Mariano made a left turn on *Via della Conciliazione* and, lo and behold, there was *St. Peter's Basilica* in all its splendor! Most people sighed in amazement. What they had seen in books and in movies was right in front of them! It was really a dream come true.

On Via della Conciliazione we found a large crowd of people rushing to St. Peter's Square. I stood on a concrete bench and shouted to my pilgrims: "Come closer. Hear me. Look at that sign on that wall; it says *Caffe San Pietro*. This place will serve as meeting point if you get lost today. Regroup here at 12:30. Now, we are going to the Pope's Audience. Look at that huge crowd; once we are in the Square there is no way and no need to stay all together. Pronto? (Ready?). Andiamo (Let's go!)" Everybody, obedient and anxious, followed me just like a flock of Canadian gees follows their leader.

First, we had to go through a light security check, and then everyone rushed to find a convenient place in the Square. The crowd was huge, impressive: there were at least 100,000 people from every corner of the world. They were all anxiously waiting to see the Pope. In the crowd, we could distinguish many large groups dressed in their national folkloric costumes; they played music and sang. Several small groups waved a banner of their parish church or a flag of their country. The view of such a crowd and its heartfelt enthusiasm was the first thing that emotionally overcame my thirty-five timid pilgrims.

At 10:30 A.M. a loud excitement was heard from the left front of the Square: dressed all in white clothes and standing on an open car, *Pope Francis* had started circulating among the crowd. Immediately, the entire Square became electrified. The cheer: "Viva il Papa!" (Long live the Pope) and applauses resounded everywhere. To have a closer look at the Pope and to take pictures, many people ran to the barriers where his mobile was going to drive. For about twenty minutes, the Pope made his way among the crowd in bright sunlight; he was smiling, cheering, greeting, touching hands and blessing. Upon seeing him, some of my people said they felt like if they were touched by an angel.

Next, the Pope climbed the steps of the Basilica and sat under a large white canopy. On both sides there were numerous cardinals, bishops, and dignitaries. Seen him up there, to most people in the Square the Pope looked only like a little white dot; but there were four huge television screens that enlarged the event and thus everyone could see and hear him quite comfortably.

After reciting a few prayers and giving a homily, the Pope greeted in their own language several groups in attendance. When their name was called, those groups cheered, clapped hands and waved their banner. At the end of the Audience the Pope recited the "Our Father" prayer in Latin and blessed the people and their religious articles, such as crucifixes and rosaries. The Audience lasted about one and half hour.

Vatican City: Pope Francis

As the Pope's Audience ended, the huge crowd left St. Peter's Square and headed for restaurants, souvenir shops or Vatican Museums. At 12:30 p.m., all my thirty-five pilgrims were in front of Café San Pietro. While standing in line for our food, the head waiter, Pino, gave us a complimentary glass of champagne, green olives, and potato chips. Lunch was good, but not cheap. Well, where in that area can you find a cheap meal?

At 1:30 p.m., we regrouped and walked back to St. Peter's Basilica. As we came through the Vatican's border gate, I told Ralph, "Stop. Go back to Italy."

"Why? What did I do wrong?" he wondered.

"You have too many sins!" Paul joked.

Ralph stood on the Italian side of the fence, right in front of us, and I, standing on the Vatican side, shook his hand across the fence and said:

"Look, Ralph, you are in Italy and I am in Vatican City. The white stone on the ground between us is *No Man's Land*."

Although we had just been in St. Peter's Square, my people had no chance of admiring it: their attention had been concentrated on the Pope. Therefore, I gave this short account of what they were seeing. "This is one of the most beautiful and most famous squares in the world. Bernini constructed it in 1656. A total of 248 columns form the *Colonnade,* which is surmounted by 140 colossal statues of saints. The colonnade looks like two outstretched arms welcoming the visitors. In the middle of the square stands the eighty-four-foot-tall *Obelisk,* transported from Egypt to Rome by the imperial legions. The Obelisk was first set in the middle of Nero's Circus and later moved to the present location. It took almost a year to erect it. Finally, it required the power of 900 men and 140 horses to raise it in position. For security reasons and under penalty of death, on the last day all workers were ordered to keep absolute silence. However, when the ropes were about to catch on fire, 'Acqua alle funi!' (water to the ropes), yelled a worker. Water was poured on the ropes and a disaster avoided. The courage of that worker was not punished, but rewarded."

I took the group to the center of St. Peter's Square and pointed out a magnificent palace rising above the right colonnade. "That is the *Pope's Palace*," I said. "Every Sunday at noon, he recites the Angelus Domini and blesses the crowd from the *second window on the top right floor.*" We took a group picture with St. Peter's Basilica in the background.

"Where is the *Sixteen Chapel* with the *holy smoke?*" Rose wanted to know.

"Rose, it is not Sixteen, but *Sistine* Chapel. They have no smoke now, but only during a pope's election." We know that during the Conclave a little stove from that Chapel billows black smoke if no pope is chosen and white smoke when a new pope is elected. I told Ann, "Look at the Colonnade to your right. How many rows of columns do you see?"

"Four."

"Now stand on this circular stone near the center of the Square and tell me how many rows you see."

"Only one! Oh, this is fantastic! What a great masterpiece of architectural symmetry!"

To enter the Basilica, we had to stand in line and go through a security check. Then, we passed in front of the *Portone di Bronzo* (Bronze Door), which is the main entrance to the Apostolic Palace. Two Swiss Guards guarded the door while dressed in colorful medieval uniforms. Then, we went through a dress code check point: two attendants made sure men wore *no shorts* and women had their *shoulders covered and wore no miniskirts.*

When we arrived at the bottom of the grand staircase, Angela lamented: "Mamma Mia, how can I go up there?"

I took her to an elevator provided for physically impaired. An attendant escorted her. I waved and told her: "I will see you at the entrance hall." We were now at the threshold *St. Peter's Basilica,* the heart of Christendom and largest and most magnificent Christian Basilica. The façade of the Basilica has huge columns and pilasters. From their top, thirteen gigantic statues of Christ, St. John the Baptist and eleven apostles look down on the Square. At the Entrance Hall, we stopped by the *Holy Door* which opens every twenty-five years and for other momentous events, such as Jubilee years. It is also called *The Door of Pardon,* because, if one meets the requirements set by the Church and walks through that door, all his/her sins are forgiven. A uniformed attendant reminded me tour guides are not allowed to give explanations inside the Basilica; therefore, I limited myself to point out the major monuments and to whisper a few things to those close to me.

A deep, spiritual feeling of holiness and reverence overwhelmed us upon entering St. Peter's Basilica. We felt as though we were entering the gates of heaven. It is impossible to describe people's emotions when entering that holy shrine for the first time. They remain speechless; some, absorbed in contemplation of its sublime beauty, reach celestial sensations, and experience an outpouring of emotional reactions, like rapid heartbeats, confusion, or a sort of ecstasy. We saw pilgrims saying prayers with their raised arms; others were on their knees; some had tears in the eyes.

A few pilgrims kept on repeating, "Oh my God!"

No wonder I lost two of my ladies in that crowd: they were frozen in a kind of spiritual ecstasy.

Yes, the architectural and artistic splendor of St. Peter's Basilica goes beyond all expectations and leaves visitors speechless, but what overwhelmingly captivates their mind is the idea they are standing on the same ground where St. Peter was crucified for his faith. The idea also amazes pilgrims they are in the same place sanctified by thousands of early Christians who went there to find the strength to endure persecution and martyrdom. Pilgrims are amazed by the thought that for some 2000 years, millions upon millions of Christians, including kings, saints, and historic figures, went to St. Peter's Basilica to worship and profess their faith. Visitors are captivated by the innumerable religious and historic events that took place inside that Basilica. They are moved by the religious devotion of so many people coming to listen to the Vicar of Christ and to seek a message of faith and hope. Yes, indeed, St. Peter's Basilica is the living and palpitating heart of Christendom, the place where faith, history, and art blend together and form a master-piece of beauty and majesty.

After a few minutes of astonishment, my people gathered around me. While standing on the centerline of the church, in front of the main entrance door, I asked Mario:

"Do you know where you are standing?"

"No, why?"

"Look at the reddish *porphyry disc* under your feet. It is a remnant of the old Basilica. Twenty-three kings knelt right there to be crowned by popes as rulers of the Holy Roman Empire. The first and most fa-mous one was King Charlemagne in 800 A.D. On Christmas night, he knelt right here to be crowned by Pope Leo III." Nick walked up to Mario, bowed down and murmured: "Hail, King Mario!"

Proceeding at a very slow pace, we started our tour of the Basilica from the right aisle. The first stop was by the Chapel of the *Pietà*. The Pieta' is a statue sculptured by Michelangelo in 1499, when he was just twenty-four years old. That work of art depicts the Virgin Mary cradling the dead body of Jesus in her lap after the crucifixion. It is the most stunning work of art inside the church and one of the most moving pieces of sculpture ever created. The white marble statue seems to be alive; the face of the Virgin, so perfectly sculptured, resembles that of a living young woman and her clothes seem to flow. In 1972, the statue was placed behind a protective glass, after being damaged with an ax by a fanatic. The Polish *Pope John Paul II* is greatly missed by the faith-ful. His tomb has recently been moved into the chapel next to La Pieta'. People stop there, bring flowers, kneel, and say a silent prayer. Nearby we saw the tomb of Queen Christina of Sweden who abdicated her throne in 1654 to convert to Catholicism.

"Oh, look at that wonderful painting right above Pope John Paul's tomb" Mary marveled.

"That represents the martyrdom of *St. Sebastian*," I whispered, but it is not a painting, it is a mosaic. In fact, if you move to a certain angle, you will see the shining little pieces of colored marble. Know there are no paintings in this Basilica; whatever looks like painting is in fact made with mosaic."

The Chapel of the *Blessed Sacrament* was next. A sign read: "Only those who wish to pray may enter". The incorrupt body of *Pope John XXIII* (dead in 1963) is displayed in a glass case beneath the altar of St. Jerome. Around the corner, we found a huge bronze statue of St. Peter Enthroned; his left foot is almost completely worn out by pilgrims touching and kissing it.

In the center of the Basilica stands the monumental bronze canopy made of four huge spiral columns called *Baldacchino*. It stands over the high altar, which sits on the site of St. Peter's tomb. It is a creation of Bernini in 1624, made with the bronze removed from the Pantheon's ceiling. Under the Baldacchino, one can see the *Papal Altar* where the Pope celebrates mass on major religious holidays.

Directly under the Papal Altar, two staircases lead down to an altar where is located the *Tomb of the Apostle St. Peter*. There are ninety-five oil lamps constantly burning above the tomb in reverence to St. Peter, the first Pope. That spot is the spiritual and physical center of the Basilica and of the Christian world. You remember the words Jesus spoke to Peter: "You are Peter and upon this rock I will build my church."

We walked around the Baldacchino and looked all the way up. The majestic *Cupola* (or Dome) by Michelangelo appeared like a huge celestial umbrella suspended into the immensity of the sky. We felt very small under it! The Cupola represents one of the greatest masterpieces of architecture, engineering and decorative art ever created. Climbing its 551 steps one gets to the very top at a height of 452 ft. From there one can enjoy lovely views of Rome.

Each of the four massive piers supporting the Dome has a niche with an enormous statue: St. Longinus, St. Helena, St. Veronica, and St. Andrew. *Longinus* was the Roman centurion who pierced Jesus' side with a lance and later became a Christian and martyr. *Helena*, the mother of the Emperor Constantine, is represented holding a large cross. *Veronica* used her veil to wipe Jesus' face on his way to Calvary.

Jesus left his image imprinted on that veil. The Apostle *Andrew* evangelized Greece and was crucified there.

Throughout the Basilica, we found many elaborate papal tombs. To know who is buried there one must read the Latin inscription on each tomb. I pointed out the glass case containing the body of Pope St. Pius X.

"How tall are you?" I asked Nick.

"6.00."

"Look at those *golden letters* up there around the Basilica's cornice. They appear quite small, but each letter is seven feet tall, taller than you!"

"Mary, stand by that Cherubim holding the holy water stoup. Look, it is twice your height!"

I took my group to the central nave and pointed out, in the marble pavement, few *brass marks* showing the length of the major churches in the world. In comparison, St. Peter's Basilica is the largest of them all.

"Remo, are we going to see the Vatican Museum now?" Laura asked.

"No, that takes a half day. You will see it in two days. Now we are going to the Catacombs. Do you know what the Catacombs are?" I asked.

Immediately, John answered, "Oh, yes. That is where the dead people lived!"

The Catacombs are underground passageways outside the walls of Rome where during the persecutions the Christians prayed and buried their loved ones. They say that, if laid in a straight line, there would be 360 miles of catacombs. However, when we refer to the *Catacombs in Vatican City*, we mean the underground, the basement of St. Peter's Basilica.

Descending to the Catacombs, we saw fragments of the old basilica built by Constantine, funeral monuments, sarcophagi, statues, busts, mosaics, inscriptions, and other important religious remains of the early Christian times. We found also many tombs of popes. We saw a small dark box containing the remains of the *Apostle St. Peter.* Most people kneel in front of it and say a prayer. While we were down there a voice on a loud speaker kept on reminding in many languages: "This is a place of prayer. Please be silent."

When we exited St. Peter's Basilica, John said, "Just to see this church was worthy a trip to Rome. One does not need to be Catholic or Christian to appreciate its artistic splendor and its religious significance. One has to be just a normal human being."

Vatican City: St. Peter's Basilica

Coming out of the Basilica, we descended the steps and saw two *Swiss Guards* standing guard at the gate entrance of the left side of the Basilica. They were dressed in blue, yellow, and red uniforms and wore a plumed helmet; they hold a halberd. Every hour on the hour they have the *Change of Guard*. We waited a few minutes to see it. The ritual was an interesting pageantry.

Nick asked, "Why Swiss Guards and not Vatican Guards?"

I explained that, when in 1527 King Charles V of Spain attacked Rome, Pope Clement VII was deserted by all his regular soldiers, except by the Swiss mercenaries. Since then the Pope knew whom to trust. There are 134 Swiss Guards; they must be Swiss citizens, Catholic, unmarried, between the ages of nineteen and thirty, of good conduct and at least 5'10" tall. They serve for two years.

At 4:30 p.m., we drove to the Basilica of *St. John in Lateran*. That is the Cathedral of the Diocese of Rome, while St. Peter's Basilica is considered the world's cathedral. Imagine: the main entrance *Bronze Door* of St. John is the same door that stood in the Roman Senate House 2000 years ago! Inside the church, we admired the marble floor, the beautiful decorations, and the elaborate gilded wooden ceiling. The central nave contains twelve niches, each has a twenty-foot-tall statue of the twelve apostles. High on the left, front side of the church, one can see a golden table behind which is kept the real *table* on which Jesus celebrated the Last Supper.

Next, we walked across the street and visited the church of *La Scala Santa*. It is a staircase with twenty-eight marble steps. Those are the same steps Jesus climbed on his way to the palace of Pontius Pilate. The steps were stained with Jesus blood. St. Helena, mother of the Emperor Constantine, had them brought to Rome in the year 326. Pilgrims can climb the steps only on their knees. They climb on wooden boards, but, through an opening in the middle of each board, one can see the original marble steps underneath. Several of my pilgrims made that devout climb.

From St. John in Lateran, we went to the nearby church of *Santa Croce in Gerusalemme* (Holy Cross of Jerusalem). It houses many relics of the Passion of the Lord. We saw *two thorns* from the Crown of Thorns, a fragment of the *True Cross*, the *pillar* to which Jesus was tied, and scourged, one *nail* from the Crucifixion and the inscription *INRI*, which was placed above the cross.

The view of the holy relics was touching. Most people sighed: "Oh, My God!" Some sobbed, a few had tears in their eyes, and others fell to their knees. When we returned to the bus, there was complete silence. People were overwhelmed by what they had just seen. That visit concluded the pilgrimage to the roots of our Christian Faith.

175

Vatican City: Swiss Guards

CHAPTER 17

WHEN IN ROME, DO AS THE ROMANS DO

We have just discovered the historic and religious heritage of Rome. However, to discover that "Eternal City" is not enough to know about its history and monuments; one must discover also its *Soul*. That is possible only if one walks through its streets, mingles with its people and observes what they *DO*. On Day Sixteen of our tour, we sat out to do exactly that.

It is important to understand here that, since our time in Rome was limited, we could *DO* only a few of the things the Romans do, but we *OBSERVED* many things they do. What exactly the Romans *DO* that others don't *DO?* The Romans of the imperial times lived by the motto, *Carpe diem* (enjoy the present day). Likewise, the modern Romans like to live the *Dolce Vita* (sweet life). That does not mean they are *fannulloni* (lazy bones); it means that, besides taking care of their duties and responsibilities, the Romans enjoy living a certain life style, characterized by a desire to relax, and enjoy of the present time without letting themselves be oppressed by the concerns of the future days. The word "Domani" (Tomorrow) is heard frequently: if you cannot do something today, don't worry, do it "domani"!

One thing the Romans *DO* for sure is to *walk,* and we certainly imitated them during that entire day. In fact, the best way to discover the

Soul of Rome is to stroll from street to street, from alley to alley and from piazza to piazza.

We started our strolling at the large *Piazza del Popolo* (People's Square*)*, which I jokingly call *Round Square,* because it is a *square,* but it is *round.* I warned my people to stick together the entire day, because there was a risk of getting lost in the crowd or in the narrow streets. Yes, my good thirty-five vacationers followed me like soldiers in a compact Roman legion. We stopped in the middle of the huge Piazza del Popolo to admire the seventy-five-foot-tall Egyptian obelisk brought to Rome by the emperor Augustus. On each of the four corners a lion spouts water from the mouth. A few of us wanted a picture sitting on a lion's back. A few horse drawn carriages waited for clients. A street musician, dressed in black pants, white shirt, red vest, and a straw hat, played a barrel organ, while a tiny monkey, in shorts with suspenders and a red and white checked shirt, held a bucket for donations. An ice cream man, wearing a white apron, served delicious *gelatos* to a group of nuns. Soon he was surrounded also by most of us. Eating gelatos is certainly one thing all Romans do very frequently! However, what tourists don't know is in the olden times Piazza del Popolo was also a place for public executions.

Next, we proceeded through *Via del Babbuino.* Like all streets in the historic downtown Rome, the Via is lined with beautiful palaces plastered with stucco of light orange color. Those imposing palaces have four, five or six floors and some have a terrace with greenery on top. All windows on the first floor are protected by heavy metal bars and thus the people inside those windows seemed to be really in jail, *behind bars.*

We walked by the Ristorante Canova. The outside tables were crowded with locals having a *cappuccino* and a *cornetto* (croissant) for breakfast. Their cappuccino with cream and cacao looked very tasty. Those people did not seem concerned about hurrying to work. On a corner-street a pretty, young gypsy woman, with a colorful, long, brownish dress and a whitish scarf, asked for money.

Paul scolded her, "Signorina, get a job!"

We passed by the statue of the *Babuino*, an ugly mythological character; his head was that of an old bearded man and the rest of the body like that of a goat. That statue gave the name to Via del Babuino. A few school children in blue uniforms ran in front of us, while their mother kept an eye on them.

"Angelo, Angelo. Dov'e'Angelo?" (where is Angelo?) shouted a concerned mother; perhaps, she suspected Angelo might be skipping school.

On a narrow cobblestone street, two pleasantly plump Italian women carried a basket full of vegetables, bread, meat, and a small bottle of wine. That meant an *open-air market* was nearby. We asked the ladies and discovered a bustling market with colorful displays of fruit, vegetables, flowers, fresh fish, baked goods, delicatessen, wine cellars, clothing, and a variety of trinkets. The locals, mostly women, were bargain hunting, socializing, and eating, as they strolled through the market. Like them, we too bought some fruit, smiled, and complimented the vendors who responded with a bow and gave some free grapes to a couple of our ladies. The visit to the market gave us a firsthand glimpse of everyday Roman life. Not only, but in that market Rose experienced what she had been warned by her friends back home. While staring at a few strange fish, she suddenly screamed, jumped a few feet ahead, and touched her behind. She thought a shark might have tried to get her! No, it was an elderly man who just snuck in the crowd and pinched her quite hard. Perhaps he was nostalgic of his good old days when Roman men used to *pinch* pretty, foreign women.

Finally, when we arrived at our first attraction of the day, I said, "We are now in *Piazza di Spagna*! (Spanish Square). The beautiful steps in front of us are the famous *Spanish Steps* you have heard so much about. They constitute the longest and widest staircase in Europe. This is the favorite spot where locals sit, bask in the sun, rest their feet, read, or simply people-watch. If you climb the 138 elegant and wide steps, you will be standing in front of *Trinita' Dei Monti Church*. From up there, you can enjoy an awesome panoramic view of Rome. Both this Piazza and these steps are named *Spanish* after the Spanish Embassy that once stood here. The steps were designed and built by Francesco De Sanctis in 1723."

"Now, look at *Via Condotti* right behind us. It is the city's most famous and fashionable street, the street that every woman adores. There are many boutiques offering gorgeous clothes with glamorous labels: Armani, Versace, Prada, Mila, Ferre, Gucci, Bulgari, Valentino, Hermes, Cartier, Fendi, and Ferragamo. The historic *Caffè Greco* is here, on the right corner; it is often visited by famous musicians, artists, philosophers, politicians, and royalty. At 11:00 a.m., be back here by this man selling roasted chestnuts right behind us. Now go and live like these Romans do."

A newlywed couple posed on the steps for professional wedding pictures. People applauded: "Auguri, Auguri" (Congratulations). The groom thanked with a handful of *confetti*.

Directly at the bottom of the steps, there is a nice and artistic fountain-shaped like a boat; it is called *Barcaccia*. It is another of Bernini's masterpieces. You can drink its fresh water; it comes straight from the mountains.

A few of my young people ran to the top of the steps and from up there they waved triumphantly to people below. My oldest people sat on the first steps, took pictures, and ate a gelato. Two ladies went on a nostalgic ride of a horse-drawn carriage; they looked like Cleopatra and Madame de Pompadour triumphantly entering the Eternal City of Rome. Karen walked along Via Condotti and was about to enter Valentino's boutique, but, upon seeing a gentleman coming out of there in a perfectly tailored blue suit and strutting like a peacock, she decided to do some window-shopping in front of Versace's store. She dreamed of wearing the red dress, the elegant purse, and the matching shining shoes she admired. She asked her husband to accompany her inside.

"Oh boy, there goes my credit card!" he objected. However, he was pleased when Karen accepted to have instead a tasty snack at Caffè Greco among artists and intellectuals. I went to find out how much a room at the luxurious Hotel de Russie costs. The lowest was $800 and the highest about $2000 euros per day. Mamma Mia!

Rome: Spanish Steps

It would have been nice to stay by the Spanish Steps for at least half day, but we were on a strict time schedule and had to discover more of Rome's *soul*. At 11:00 a.m., I took the roll call, and then we walked again. A little further down, we greeted the statue of the Immaculate Conception situated on top of a column; then we proceeded slowly along Via di Propaganda.

In a small old square, we saw a group of elderly men playing cards. We noticed that, any time a woman walked by, all heads turned and humorous comments were made. Further down, an old woman sat on a bench conversing with her friend. Using both hands, she was eagerly trying to make a point about something. Another elderly woman sat by a fountain; she kept a watchful eye on her grandson riding a tricycle. In the corner of the square, almost hidden from the tourist crowd, a grey-haired man, sitting on a makeshift bicycle and pedaling fast, chanted some old songs while sharpening knives and scissors. He gladly posed for a picture with Betty and then with his dusty index finger he pointed to his cheek for a kiss. Betty did it immediately, but later she wiped her lips.

Rome is full of surprises; you breathe history all the time. One can find a great ancient monument at every turn and become emotional at any moment. We suddenly came upon the remains of a 2000-year-old aqueduct, almost completely buried between two modern palaces. Then, we stopped in front of Palazzo del Bufalo and, above the entrance door, I pointed out a sculpture depicting the fierce face of what seemed to be a wolf. It had a Latin inscription: "Cum feris ferus." Nobody could give me the correct translation, even those who had studied Latin. Finally, I explained it means: "I am mean with mean people."

Two devout, older ladies descended the steps of San Andrea Church. Their heads were covered with black veils, and their right hands carried prayer books. The women were totally unconcerned about the crowds on the street.

At an outside flower shop a man had just bought a red rose and placed it on his woman's hair, while giving her a kiss. That inspired John to do the same to his wife Karen. An elder man, driving a tricycle full of water melons, nervously tried to make his way in a crowded side street. Two other elder men played chess on a small table; they were so concentrated on the game they did not care about people stopping by. A young, romantic couple riding a "Vespa" scooter wormed through the crowd despite the "Vigile" (Policeman) whistling at them. It seemed Gregory Peck and Audrey Hepburn were back in Rome for their "Roman Holiday".

We stopped at the busy *Via Del Tritone* and watched an entertaining scene. A young man with a motorcycle had slightly hit the rear of a shiny new Fiat car. The traffic came to a halt and the two drivers kept on arguing, cussing, and threatening, until a policeman restored order. The word *Vaffanculo* (Up yours!) was heard a few times. Yes, Romans drive fast; often they ignore the traffic signs and have frequent accidents. Well, when in Rome tourists are not expected to drive or use the word 'Vaffanculo', as Romans do!"

We entered Via Stamperia and walked to the end of the street. Bingo, there was *Trevi Fountain,* the most beautiful fountain in the world! Water cascading with a cheerful splashing could be seen and heard from all parts of the fountain. The sight and the sounds of that magical fountain filled everybody's heart with joy.

When my people saw it, they sighed, "Oh, it is so beautiful! It is magic! It is romantic!" They began to sing, *"Three coins in a Fountain... Make it mine..."*

Bernini and Nicola Salvi made Trevi Fountain in 1762. The water that flows there is carried by an aqueduct that has been in existence for more than 2,000 years. About 17 million gallons of water per day flow through that architectural masterpiece. Oh, yes, that fountain has been an inspiration for many artists, poets, and musicians. It is often featured in movies, especially in *La Dolce Vita* with Anita Ekberg, in the *Roman Holiday* and in Respighi's symphony *The Fountains of Rome*. The French writer Stendhal called it, "The most celebrated of all the fountains in the world".

Lovers find Trevi Fountain very romantic, especially at night with the soft lighting. They say, if you throw a coin in that lovely fountain, you will return to Rome for sure. Throw two coins and you will fall in love with an Italian man/woman. Throw three coins and you will marry him/her! To make sure the coins will work you must stand with your back to the fountain and, with the right hand over your right shoulder, throw the coins in the water. It is no wonder that some 4000 euros per day are thrown into that fountain!

Standing in front of the fountain, I announced there would be an hour and a half of free time to enjoy the scene, shop for souvenirs and have lunch. "Let us regroup at 1:00 p.m. by this Farmacia. Have fun!"

Everybody rushed to the fountain. Carmela, overly anxious to toss her coins, stumbled on a stone, fell, and got hurt. A handsome Italian man from a nearby bar came with some ice and helped her kindly; he remained with her for a while. She was very pleased, began to flirt with him and, of course, he reciprocated. When she threw her coins into the fountain she told us:

"I believe those coins really work!"

Rome: Trevi Fountain

If a tourist wants to really discover the palpitating heart of Rome, he should spend some time in the narrow streets around Trevi Fountain. There, one can find restaurants, outdoor cafés with small round tables, souvenir shops, and people everywhere. The air is filled with the delicious aroma of fresh spaghetti sauce and fresh bread from the bakery. Well-dressed Romans can be seen enjoying their steaming hot pasta, meatballs, pizza, and other mouthwatering food and delicious wine. No rush: people relax and savor every bite of food and every sip of wine. I saw tables with a party of eight, four, and two people. At a small table, I noticed a pretty, but lone, woman. With a hand, she fed crumbs to a couple of birds and with her eyes she examined every gentleman passing by. She was apparently daydreaming.

During our free time, I went to visit my nearby Alma Mater, the prestigious *Gregorian University*, where I had been a student in the early 1960s. When I returned to the Trevi Fountain area I caught sight of a few of my people. I believe somehow each of them tried to *DO* something the *Romans* were doing. Mario and Bruno stood at a bar, smiling, and sipping a cappuccino. Using a tiny dictionary and their hands, they tried to speak Italian with the waiter. Sandra and Betty fell in love with a nice purse displayed in a store. Upon seeing me walking by, they grabbed my hand and took me to the store to help speak Italian with the clerk. Laura and Tony asked a policeman for directions to the nearby Quirinale Palace, which is the Residence of the President of Italy. Peter and Luisa had never met before coming on the tour, but now they were more than just good friends; they were holdings hands and sharing an ice cream. Later, they tossed coins in the fountain and exchanged a warm kiss. I enjoyed a delicious *panino* from my favorite *Antico Forno*, right in front of Trevi Fountain.

At 1:00 p.m., we regrouped and walked along *Via dei Muratti*, crowded with people, mimes, and stands filled with all kinds of souvenirs. Carefully and all together, we crossed the busy *Via del Corso*. We proceeded among huge modern palaces and, suddenly in Piazza di Pietra, we came in front of the remains of the humongous *Temple of the Emperor Hadrian* with enormous columns. That temple is now used as seat of Stock Exchange.

Vincent got our attention when he shouted, "Holy smoke, look up there!" He had spotted a pretty brunette on the third floor. She was softly singing while hanging laundry on a clothes line tied to the neighbor's window. Vincent waved at her and she blew a kiss to him.

A few steps further, I invited everyone to go inside the 500-year-old Church of *St. Ignazio* (Ignatius), the founder of the Jesuit Order. "Give a quick look at the many marvelous paintings and sculptures. If this church could be moved to America, it would be one of the greatest tourist attractions. Rome is full of such wonderful churches," I said.

The street next to St. Ignazio is *Via Pasta* and the one after that is *Via Pastini* (Little Pasta). Both streets are very picturesque and have many restaurants and outdoor cafés. One restaurant was called *Er Faciolaro* (The Beans' Man). The restaurant, Arcano, displayed on a window a mouthwatering dish of pasta and a glass of red wine. A waiter solicited people to stop there for lunch. Among those enjoying lunch, we noticed a few business men reading a newspaper and sipping an espresso. They were completely indifferent to the crowd of tourists walking right in front of their tables.

On Via del Seminario, a store called Bartolucci sells all kinds of artistic wooden clocks. The store has an outside green bench with a tall statue of Pinocchio wearing green shorts, a red shirt, and a large white collar. When I saw a few children sitting with Pinocchio and their mother taking a picture, I said:

"Let us do what these Roman children are doing!"

Surprise, several of my *children* sat with Pinocchio, touched his nose, laughed, and had their picture taken!

On the wall of a palace, a little further down, we saw a large plaque listing local young soldiers who died during the last two World Wars. Another plaque, dated February 9, 1743, warned that, under severe penalty, it was prohibited to dump garbage there. As we passed by the shop of a shoemaker we could smell handmade leather shoes. We saw an elderly woman sitting by a door and keeping an eye on her two grandchildren chasing each other on the street.

At the end of Via dei Pastini, we suddenly went back in time of 2000 years, as we came face-to-face with an enormous old building.

"It is Castle San Angelo! No, it is the temple of Jupiter," said Rose and Luigi.

It was neither. It was the *Pantheon*, the temple dedicated to *All Gods* (in Greek, *pan* = all, and *theon* = gods).

The Pantheon is a masterpiece of the Roman architecture; it is also one of the most famous and best preserved monuments of the imperial times. Built in 27 B.C., the Pantheon stands just as it was then. Its dome is still the largest in the world. Over its magnificent Portico we can see the original Latin inscription: "M. Agrippa. L.F. Cos. Tertium Fecit" (Marcus Agrippa, son of Lucius, consul for the third time, built it). Looking at the huge monolithic columns of the Pantheon, looking at its gigantic bronze door, at the artistic ceiling and at its perfect symmetrical lines, one wonders: "How did they build such an amazing structure 2000 years ago?"

The Barbarians attempted to tear the Pantheon down; in fact, we can see the grooves they made in the columns with chains and ropes. In 609 A.D., the Pantheon was consecrated as Christian church and that prevented it from being plundered over the centuries.

The Pantheon has no windows and the only light penetrates from the *Oculus* (Eye), a thirty-foot circular opening on the very top of the ceiling. A legend says the Oculus was made by a ferocious devil, who, during the consecration of the temple, escaped by drilling a hole with his horns on the top of the ceiling. The legend also says many people complained of being assaulted by demons whenever they walked past the Pantheon.

The Pantheon has influenced numerous buildings in the world. Just think of the many American churches, city halls, universities, libraries, court houses, national galleries, memorials, and state capitols, including the Capitol building in Washington, D.C. They are all modeled after that Roman marvel. Inside the Pantheon, on the right side, one can see the tomb of *King Vittorio Emanuele II* who united Italy in 1870. On the left are the tomb of his son, *Umberto*, and that of queen, *Margherita*. The great painter, *Raphael*, is buried there too, under the statue of a Madonna.

I gave my people thirty minutes of free time to explore the prestigious Pantheon. At regrouping time, I could not find them. Rather nervous, I went back inside, but had no luck. I finally found them on a corner street. They were watching a clown dressed like Charley Chaplin: the clown captivated them just as much as the Roman children were! We waited till the end of the show before exploring the rest of Rome.

Soon, we noticed the street traffic was much lighter, most taxi drivers were snoozing, smaller stores were closed and the streets had only foreign visitors. It seemed life had come to a halt. Why? Well, at that time, the Romans observe their traditional mid-day *riposo* (rest). Yes, at about 1:00 p.m. government offices and schools end their working day; most shops low the shutters and lock the doors so owners and employees can go home for lunch and take a nap. Those places reopen at about 3:30 p.m. After several hours on our feet, we would have loved to *DO* what those Romans were doing, but how? Where? No, this time we could not *do what they did.* We had to be content *observing* or rather learning what they were doing!

When we walked in front of the 500-year-old *Palazzo Madama,* Antonietta said: "Remo, why are all those soldiers around this palace? They scare me with their machine guns!" "This is the seat of the modern Italian Senate House. Don't worry, the soldiers are for security."

By Palazzo Madama about twenty young Franciscan monks crossed the street in front of us. The wind made their robe billow like sails. They seemed to be mumbling some Latin prayer and with their right hands they held rosaries made of large wooden beads. The monks were completely disinterested in the material beauty of the Eternal City. A few steps along the Corso del Rinascimento and then we arrived to one of Rome's most famous piazza.

"Oh, yes, yes. This is it," Ann nervously stammered.

"What is it?" asked Ralph.

"I don't know. I cannot remember!"

"Remo knows; he will tell us."

"Yes, Remo knows," I said, pointing to my nose. "This beautiful baroque square is *Piazza Navona,* the most romantic and charming piazza in the world. It stands on the exact place where, about 1900 years ago, the Emperor Domitianus built a Stadium for horse races. Today, the stadium is buried twenty feet below the current street level. This Square is embellished with splendid palaces and three monumental fountains; the one in the center is called *Fontana dei Quattro Fiumi* (Fountain of the Four Rivers), because it represents the Nile, Ganges, Danube, and Rio de la Plata. It is another masterpiece of Bernini, built in 1651. Look at the graceful St. Agnes Church; I recommend you visit it. In a little chapel on the left side, you will find the skull of the Saint; she was decapitated for her faith during the persecutions against the Christians. History says before being killed, she was stripped nude, but her hair miraculously grew to protect her modesty."

"This bustling Piazza is the favorite place for Romans to enjoy themselves. They come here for a coffee, to meet friends, have a gelato, take their children, and dogs for a stroll and watch people passing by. You should walk all around the Square, look at the numerous sculptures in each fountain, see the street artists, street musicians, mimes, and some puppet show. Make sure you eat some good pizza and ice cream, for which this Square is renowned. At 5:00 p.m., regroup in front of this Fountain of Four Rivers. This is your last chance to do what Romans do. Now go, My Romans, go!"

There were many outdoor restaurants in Piazza Navona; they were all packed with locals and foreigners. Two men, dressed in Italian folkloric clothes, strolled by the tables, and serenading romantic couples; one man had an accordion and the other a guitar.

During my free time, I went to the nearby church of San Filippo Neri, where I resided while attending the Gregorian University in the early 1960s. Padre Peppino was still there, much older but in good health.

Shortly before regrouping, we noticed Piazza Navona became increasingly crowded with locals. It was time for their traditional and favorite pastime, the *Passeggiata* (evening gentle stroll), which takes place in every Italian city and town from about five to seven p.m. During the Passeggiata, one can see well-dressed individuals slowly walking and greeting their friends and acquaintances. Romantic couples, arm-in-arm, do window-shopping. Families walk with their dogs on leashes and their children riding tricycles. Here and there groups of men can be heard talking about politics, business, the latest news, or sports. Young mothers, pushing strollers with their babies, chat with other mothers and watch mimes, a puppet show or listen to musicians.

It is interesting to watch the Romans do their *passeggiata*: everyone checks out everybody's clothes and manners; they all try to impress. They do care to "*vedere e farsi vedere*" (to see and be seen), to do "*Bella figura*" (to look good) and to show that life treats them well. There is a real art in doing the evening passeggiata!

After that, everyone goes home for dinner. For some Romans, the passeggiata serves also as incentive for a good dinner in a *trattoria* with their family or friends. There they spend hours savoring their appetizing antipasto, spaghetti, chicken, wine, and the company they keep. In fact, for Romans to eat well, live well, and do *bella figura* means they are somebody and have a *gusto* for good living.

During their free time at Piazza Navona, my tired tourists would have loved to do a *passeggiata,* but time did not allow. However, they were content to *observe* that pageantry, for observing and being observed is what the Passeggiata is all about.

Rome: Navona Square

As we started walking again, Laura whined, "My feet are killing me!"

Unfortunately, we had to walk for about ten more minutes. Proceeding north of Piazza Navona, we turned left and stopped by an enormous stone gate laying some thirty feet below the ground level. That was the entrance *Gate to the Stadium of the Emperor Domitianus.*

A very short walk on Via Zanardelli took us to the left bank of Tiber River, along Longotevere Tor di Nona. The question "Where is our bus?" was on everybody's mind.

Mariano came within minutes, and we greeted him: "Ciao, Capitano Mariano. Glad to see you!"

Resting in our comfortable seats, for a brief time we drove along the Tiber River. A tourist boat was slowly moving in the water.

"What kind of trees are those along the river?" enquired Luigi.

"Those are sycamore trees," I explained.

Upon seeing a couple passionately kissing under the shade of a sycamore tree, Angela muttered, "Wow, look at that! I bet those are '*seek amore*' (seek love) trees!"

We passed in front of the *Italian Supreme Court* and then drove by the enormous *Castle Sant'Angelo*. That Castle was built in 126 A.D. as a funerary *mausoleum* for the Emperor Hadrian, his family, and many other emperors. Later, the Barbarians threw their bones in the Tiber River and used the mausoleum as fortress. Through the centuries, the castle was used also as papal residence and prison; now it is a museum. In the year 590 a terrible plague sowed death in Rome. During a religious procession to end the epidemic everybody saw an angel sheathing his sword on top of the mausoleum. The Romans interpreted it as a sign the plague had ended. In fact, it was over and they renamed the mausoleum *Castle Sant'Angelo*.

Yes, our feet needed a rest, but what an educational and rewarding day we had! Everyone fell in love with the Romans' lifestyle.

Paul even bragged: "As soon as I get home, I will live like the Romans do!"

At Hotel Antonella, we enjoyed a superb dinner and some local wines, just like the *Romans do*.

CHAPTER 18

THE GRAND FINALE

The Latin, Italian, and Spanish name for Rome is *Roma*. Reading the name backwards, it spells *Amor*, which means *Love* in those same languages. Yes, Rome is Love! Because of its historic, cultural, artistic, and religious significance, one cannot help falling in love with the Eternal City. It has a magic attraction and an energy that makes all who visit Rome want to return.

In the morning of Day Sixteen of our tour, we woke up to a bright sunshine and a wonderful breeze. At breakfast, I told my vacationers:

"You have one more day to live like Romans do. Let's go to the Vatican Museums and then we will conclude our memorable trip with another super square meal. Is everyone coming?" Only one couple preferred to stay at the hotel; the other thirty-three responded:

"Yes, we are coming!"

Antonietta said the prayer and Captain Mariano started the bus. Since we had about thirty minutes to ride, I asked if anyone had a story or a joke to tell. Marc volunteered to tell this story.

Antonio was an Italian-American living in Philadelphia. He had a friend, Mike the barber. Now and then, Antonio told Mike he was going on a trip to Italy, but his friend always discouraged him and said it was a waste of time and money. The week before leaving, Antonio announced: "Barber, I am going and I will even see the Pope. Give me the best haircut you can." "The Pope? Ah, you will see him from a mile away! Stay home."

Antonio went to Italy and then reported to his friend that everything was perfect. He added, "I saw the Pope very close. He even spoke to me!"

"Really? What did he say?"

"Imagine: while he was walking among the crowd on St. Peter's Square, he came straight to me, put his hand on my head, began to laugh and said, 'My son, who gave you that lousy haircut?'"

Mariano dropped us off at Piazza Risorgimento, near the Vatican Museums. I told people, "Now you have a free day, however, if you have never been to the Vatican Museums, I strongly suggest you go there. Regroup in front of Café San Pietro at 1:30 p.m."

A young couple went on their own, perhaps to renew their love vows at Trevi Fountain. Another couple decided to go back to the Colosseum and to Caesar's Palace. The others followed me to the museums.

Mary asked, "Could I skip the museums and see the Sistine Chapel?"

"Yes, you can, but you still have to get the same ticket. The Chapel is at the very end. Once you are inside the Museums, keep on walking, or ask the attendants to direct you there."

The line to the entrance to the Vatican Museums can be one-hour long or much shorter, it depends on the day of the week and on the events going on. That day we barely waited twenty minutes.

What are the Vatican Museums? They are the most important complex of museums in the world. They are filled with countless, priceless, and most beautiful works of art. Inside, one can find the best masterpieces of the Roman and Renaissance period as well works of art from Italy, Greece, Egypt, and other ancient civilizations. If one wants to look at each artifact in detail, it would take at least a month to complete the tour. Most tourists walk slowly, look here and there and in about two and half hours can have a general idea of the content of the museums. With an *audio guide*, it is possible to learn more, although that takes longer.

Specifically, what can we see in the Vatican Museums? Impossible to list everything here! Let's just say we can see statues, busts, torsos, mosaics, paintings, sculptures, ancient sarcophagi, mummies, ornaments, tapestries, frescoes, and figures of animals. There are also countless geographical maps, old vehicles, contemporary art, masks, ancient books and documents, sacred vestments, scientific instruments, funeral urns, bronze and gold objects, candelabra, glass work, rings, necklaces, papyri, ancient manuscripts, incunabula, etc. It is overwhelming!

How many paintings and statues are in there? Too many to mention! Made by whom? The most celebrated artists of the ancient period made them. How much are they worth? They are priceless.

The vision of all those artistic objects is great indeed, however, the crown jewel of the Vatican Museums is the famous *Sistine Chapel*. Built in 1508 by Pope Sixtus IV, it has been used as papal private chapel and, for the past 500 years, as *Conclave* to elect new popes. We know about the *black or white smoke* coming out of that Chapel during the Pope's election.

What makes the Sistine Chapel so famous is its numerous and wonderful frescoes painted by the world's most famous artists, especially by Raphael, Bernini, and Botticelli. However, what all visitors long to see in there is the *Last Judgment* and the biblical scenes painted on the *Ceiling* by *Michelangelo*. The most admired scenes are those depicting the "Creation of Man", the story of "Adam and Eve", the "Fall", and "Noah". Imagine: he painted them while lying on his back, with paint dripping in his eyes and he did it when he was in his sixties. It took him seven years to complete the work. One should watch the movie *Agony and Ecstasy* or *In the Fisherman's Shoes* to understand exactly how Michelangelo created that masterpiece. Those movies show also how anxious Pope Sixtus was to see the chapel completed.

"When will you finish?" the Pope kept asking.

"When I am done," Michelangelo answered.

"And when will you be done?"

"When I finish!"

Many of Michelangelo's paintings in the Sistine Chapel depict naked people. A few cardinals objected as being unfit for a religious chapel. The master of ceremonies Biagio da Cesena was particularly critical. Michelangelo retaliated by painting his face with long donkey's ears and placing him among people in hell. Biagio complained to the Pope.

"Holy Father, order him to remove me from hell."

"Sorry," replied the Pope, "I have the power to remove people from purgatory, but not from hell!"

Due to the large crowd, tour guides are not allowed to give explanations inside the Sistine Chapel. People aren't even allowed to talk. In fact, a loud speaker constantly reminds the visitors to keep silence. I limited myself to silently point out a few paintings to those close to me.

Vatican City, Sistine Chapel: Creation of Man

At 1:30 p.m., we were back at Caffé San Pietro. We said *Arrivederci* to Vatican City, to Castle San Angelo and to Tiber River. Then, we passed by the *Basilica of San Paolo,* where the Apostle was decapitated for his faith. Next, we drove on Via Marconi and arrived at a country restaurant called *Lo Convento* (The Convent). It was a rustic place built on the ruins of an old convent. There was a large dining room inside and a smaller one outside, in a barn surrounded by pine trees.

Everybody was surprised when we entered the restaurant: the waiters were dressed as *Franciscan monks*! They were to be addressed as "Brother Roberto, Brother Giovanni and Brother Antonio". The *brothers* were very kind and served a delicious dish of appetizers with cheese, olives, prosciutto, artichokes, and salami. Then they served pasta with a tasty, red sauce. Some men ate three dishes of pasta! Next, we had fried chicken, fresh salad, and French fries. We drank all mineral water and red and white wine we wanted.

I borrowed a monk's robe, called Mario over and dressed him as a Franciscan. He covered his head with the hood, took a big pitcher of wine and began serving. I called everybody's attention:

"Now, Brother Giuseppe is going to serve a special wine." One can imagine people laughing and teasing when they found out who Bother Giuseppe was! Ice cream, cake, and coffee concluded our last *square meal*. It was a joy for me to see my thirty-five *New Romans* happy, singing, laughing, and joking on their way back to the bus!

 One would think, after that gorgeous meal at Lo Convento, my happy people would not eat dinner at the hotel. Wrong! At 8:30 p.m., everybody was in the dining room. They ate another mouth-watering meal and had more free wine. I announced the *mileage contest:*

everyone wrote down the total number of miles they believed our bus traveled from the beginning to the end of our tour. Each participant had to give one euro. Sandra won the contest and received the money. After dinner, we lined up on the beautiful staircase of our hotel and took one final *group picture*. Then, some people had an after-dinner drink at the bar, while others hugged and exchanged addresses.

The most heartening outcome of our tour was that, at the beginning, my thirty-five vacationers did not know each other, but soon they became *buddies* and now they laughed and reminisced about the greatest adventure of their lives. Some were even crying, sad to leave the good friends they had made. Captain Mariano made generous tips and received many hugs for his kind services. Roberta, the hotel manager, came to bid us farewell.

Rome: our unforgettable tour ends with a celebration!

The next morning, the return flight was at 10:15 a.m. That meant we had to be at the airport by 8:00 a.m., had to leave the hotel at 7:30 a.m., have breakfast at 6:30 and get up at 5:30. There was an air of sadness on the bus: we were sorry our great time in Italy was over. Antonietta said a special thanksgiving prayer and Mariano drove us to Fiumicino Airport.

I kindly thanked each person for coming on the tour and gave some helpful information about checking in at the airport. "You will find a lot of people there, but take it easy because time wise we are doing fine. *Rush slowly*! Follow the instructions given by the airport personnel and you will be okay. When you get back home, for the next couple of days you will wake up at about 2:00 a.m. You will think it is time to get up, but then you will be glad to go back to your dreams. Ladies, watch your husband while he sleeps: he might still be chewing the good pasta he had in Italy or waving to some pretty woman on a balcony. Grazie. Buon Viaggio and may God bless all of you."

Immediately, some people sang: *Arrivederci, Roma. Goodbye, Au revoir.*

At the entrance of *Fiumicino International Airport,* a colossal bronze statue of Leonardo da Vinci greeted us. Mariano took us to Terminal 5. I helped a couple of elderly ladies with their baggage; the others followed me and stood in line by the check-in counter. Every single person hugged and thanked me for a wonderful tour. I remained in the airport waving until the last of my dear *sheep* was gone.

When I returned to the bus, I told Mariano, "Andiamo" (Let us go). Neither one of us felt like saying anything; we were very sad. After two weeks of fun and good company, I suddenly felt like a shepherd who had just lost his beloved flock. I looked at the clear and sunny sky and said: "Lord, Grazie. Please protect them on their return flight." That concluded one of my many wonderful tours to Italy.

I did not return with the group; I had extended my air ticket for two weeks, so I could spend some time with my ninety-eight-year-old *Mamma Lucia* in Abruzzo. When I returned home to the USA, I found many "*Thank-You*" letters from my good people. The letters said:

"Remo, thank you so much for the most wonderful tour I ever had."

"It was a trip of a lifetime."

"It was a dream trip."

"Wonderful time and a lot of laughs. Grazie."

"The best time of my life."

"Italy has become part of my soul."

"You made the old country come alive."

"We enjoyed every single bit of it."

"I will never forget it. It was a blast."

"This was the most enjoyable tour. We all had a great time."

"I am so grateful for the beautiful memories of Italy etched in my heart. Blessings to you."

My Dear Good People, Thank You, Grazie, Merci, Danke Schon, Au revoir, Gracias, Gratias vobis ago.

http://www.italianheritagetours.com/